Introduction

In 1977 the UK's fixed-wing airframe companies were merged to become British Aerospace (BAe). The newly-formed company inherited a number of military programmes; the Tornado, Jaguar, Harrier and Hawk which assured steady work for the military aircraft sector of the organisation. The civil sector was less secure as its major products were mostly at the end of their production cycle. To maintain BAe's position in this sector, the 125 and Jetstream were further developed, the company rejoined the Airbus consortium and BAe146 received the go-ahead.

BAe merged with GEC-Marconi to become BAE SYSTEMS in 1999, which altered the balance of its portfolio. By 2006 the company had completely withdrawn from civil aircraft manufacture and had evolved into a much broader-based defence contractor which was also a major manufacturer of warships and military vehicles. It remains a major military aircraft manufacturer as it is a lead partner in the Eurofighter Typhoon and in the F-35 Lightning 2, besides producing the Hawk trainer and investing heavily in innovative military UAV programmes.

British Aerospace's combat aircraft and the EAP (Experimental Aircraft Programme) prior to the advent of the Eurofighter Typhoon. From the front; EAP ZF534, Hawk 100 Demonstrator ZA101, Hawk 200 prototype ZH200, Harrier GR5, Sea Harrier FRS1, Tornado GR4 and Tornado F3.
(BAE SYSTEMS via Warton Heritage)

Acknowledgements: I would like to acknowledge the assistance provided to me by Dave Ward and Bernard Page of BAE North West Heritage, Warton, George Jencks of Avro Heritage, Woodford, Peter Hotham of BAE Brough, George Rollo, Ken Haynes, Barry Guess and Trevor Friend of BAE SYSTEMS Archive, Farnborough. **Cover images:** BAE Systems.

Author: Stephen Skinner
steveskinner@ntlworld.com

Advertisement Sales: Andrew Mason
Tel +44 (0) 1780 755131
andrew.mason@keypublishing.com
Group Marketing Manager: Martin Steele
Design: Rob Terry, design@focusedondesign.co.uk
Production Manager: Janet Watkins
Ad Production Manager: Debi McGowan

Group Editor: Nigel Price
Commercial Director: Ann Saundry
Managing Director/Publisher: Adrian Cox
Executive Chairman: Richard Cox
Distributed by: Seymour Distribution Ltd
2 Poultry Avenue, London, EC1A 9PP, UK.
Tel +44 (0) 20 7429 4000
Printed by: Warners (Midland) PLC,
The Maltings, Manor Lane,
Bourne, Lincs PE10 9PH, UK.
ISSN - 978 1 912205 03 5

Published by: Key Publishing Ltd.
PO Box 100, Stamford, Lincs, PE9 1XO, UK.
Tel: +44 (0) 1780 755131

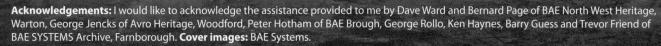

Contents

CONTENTS

The first Typhoon and the first Hawk for Oman were rolled out at Warton on 4 May 2017. They are temporarily registered ZR411 and ZB123 respectively. Oman ordered 12 Typhoons and eight Hawks in December 2012. *(BAE SYSTEMS)*

From British Aerospace to BAE SYSTEMS 1977- 2017

The formation of British Aerospace - Europe's largest aerospace company

Today's BAE Systems is a very different business to the British Aerospace that was formed by the UK Government in 1977 and was then Europe's largest aircraft, missile and space manufacturer. It was only briefly state-owned and by 1985 it was entirely in private ownership. Today's BAE SYSTEMS is a defence contractor providing aircraft, warships, tanks, electronics, cyber security and intelligence. Its key markets are Australia, the UK, India, Saudi Arabia and the USA. It also has a substantial holding in MBDA, a multi-national missile manufacturer.

From nationalisation to privatisation

The Nationalisation Bill had a stormy passage through Parliament but came into force on 29 April 1977 with the formation of state-owned British Aerospace encompassing the British Aircraft Corporation (BAC), the aviation and dynamics divisions of Hawker Siddeley and Scottish Aviation (SAL) in its entirety.

Just like Hawker Siddeley with its large portfolio of aircraft and guided missiles, Vickers and GEC, which jointly owned BAC would have preferred to retain ownership of their highly profitable organisations. The directors and shareholders of these companies were aggrieved when they received compensation they regarded as grossly inadequate.

Scottish Aviation based at Prestwick was far smaller than these two giants. It

BRITISH AEROSPACE working for Britain's future prosperity

◄ British Aerospace logo 1977-1999.
(BAE SYSTEMS)

had a dwindling amount of work and the workforce had been virtually halved to 1,400 just prior to nationalisation. So, except for Scottish Aviation the other companies taken over were showing a profit and had healthy order books.

The new grouping had 59,000 employees working in aircraft manufacture and 17,000 working on missiles and space products.

From part to full-privatisation

In May 1979, the Labour Government was replaced by a Conservative Government led by Margaret Thatcher which had pledged to privatise British Aerospace. In January 1980, the company was made a public concern and the following month the state sold 51.25% of the shares. To general surprise in January 1985 the Government announced that the

The BAe 146 prototype G-SSSH airborne on its maiden flight from Hatfield on 3 September 1981. This aircraft later became the 146-300 prototype re-registered as G-LUXE. It is now a meteorological research aircraft based at Cranfield, Bedfordshire. *(BAE SYSTEMS)*

remainder of British Aerospace would be sold off, though a 'Golden share' was retained so that the Government could veto foreign control of the firm and stated that the chairman and chief executive must be British. In May 1985 the sale took place and BAe was fully in private hands.

BAe's aircraft manufacturing sites, then and now

At formation, British Aerospace inherited many sites across the UK but very few of these remain today. As BAE SYSTEMS, the organisation has changed considerably in emphasis with many other plants in the UK, for instance in Telford and Cambridge and elsewhere in the world such as Sterling Heights, Michigan, USA where BAE SYSTEMS Combat Vehicles HQ is based.

In the 1980s there were closures of BAe factories at Bitteswell in Leicestershire, Holme-on-Spalding-Moor in Yorkshire, Hurn in Dorset and Weybridge, Surrey. In the early 1990s Hawker's factory at Kingston, Surrey and the famous former De Havilland Hatfield plant in Hertfordshire followed suit.

Dunsfold, Surrey, was closed in 2000, Broughton and Filton were passed to Airbus in 2006 and in 2011 and 2012, two famous former Hawker Siddeley (Avro) sites at Woodford and Chadderton in Cheshire were closed.

The company's strategy was to sell off its valuable sites, especially those in southern England and redevelop them, generally very profitably. The sites still involved with aircraft manufacture and support for BAE are Warton, Samlesbury, Brough and Prestwick.

Warton, Lancs., carries out final assembly of Hawk (since 2010) and Typhoon. Research and manufacture of UAV, UCAV testbeds, e.g. Mantis and Taranis. Warton

➤ **The BAe Jetstream 31 prototype G-JSSD was a conversion of a Handley Page built Jetstream. It made its first flight from Prestwick on 23 March 1980.** *(BAE SYSTEMS)*

is BAE Systems flight test centre.
Samlesbury Lancs., produces components for Hawk, Typhoon, F-35 Lightning 2.
Brough, Yorks., provides Hawk support.
Prestwick, Ayrshire, supports over 650 BAE civil aircraft i.e., Jetstream 31/32, Jetstream 41, ATP, HS748 and BAe 146/Avro RJ families operated by over 190 customers in 70 countries.

BAe's missile and space manufacturing sites

The newly formed BAe Dynamics brought together BAC Guided Weapons and

Hawker Siddeley Dynamics. BAe established two subsidiaries, one dealing with Space Systems and the other Guided Weapons. Four pre-nationalisation sites remain in the aerospace business. The former Hawker Siddeley plant at Lostock is now part of MDBA, as are the former BAC plants at Filton and Stevenage. The remaining aerospace site at Stevenage is now part of Airbus Space and Defence.

British Aerospace's civil strategy

The new company was confronted by the need to derive a civil airliner strategy. The ➤

Air France Airbus A300 F-BVGA at London Heathrow in 1974. It was the fifth Airbus A300 built. *(BAE SYSTEMS)*

major question was whether it should rejoin the Airbus consortium. It also needed to decide whether to invest in developments of the One-Eleven, relaunch the suspended HS146, develop a 748 replacement and the Jetstream and fund new marks of the 125-executive jet.

146 and Jetstream

Before deciding about Airbus, the BAe Board first considered the case of the HS146. This was a 70-100 seat jetliner proposal that had been launched by Hawker Siddeley in 1973 but suspended by them in the following year. The Government had funded the company to maintain low-scale project work to keep the design in being until nationalisation. Despite earlier misgivings, the Board went ahead with the146 in July 1978. With the go-ahead for the 146 the One-Eleven was not developed further, although continued production of the One-Eleven was licenced to continue in Romania.

At the end of the year BAe also agreed to re-launch of the Jetstream 31, a 19-seater twin-turboprop feederliner. This was a limited go-ahead and it was not until January 1981 that the Board finally approved the production of the first batch of twenty aircraft at Prestwick.

Airbus or Boeing?

Airbus Industrie was formed in 1967 to design and build a 300-seater airliner. Hawker Siddeley and Sud Aviation had been the major partners providing 37.5% of the costs and sharing work in those proportions, while Deutsche Airbus provided the remaining 25% of the finance and the work. This was a Government-sponsored project and in 1968 Britain withdrew from it, putting

∧ BAe 125-800 made its maiden flight in primer from Broughton on 26 May 1983. It was repainted for its ceremonial roll-out and demonstration flight as N800BA the following week. *(Ken Haynes)*

Airbus in crisis. Notwithstanding the UK's withdrawal, the consortium continued and Hawker Siddeley, tasked with building the wing remained in the project as a major sub-contractor. With nationalisation this contract now fell within BAe's remit.

In February 1978 as BAe deliberated on its strategy, waters were muddied when Boeing offered BAe the opportunity to build the wings of its new 200-seater 757 twin-jet. Boeing argued that BAe would find it more profitable to form an alliance with them than with Airbus. Rolls-Royce which was supplying the RB211 for the 757 also applied pressure on the Government and BAe to work with Boeing.

However British Aerospace believed that Airbus offered the best technological and commercial deal and resisted Government pressure to sign a deal with Boeing. The nationalised British Aerospace formally became an Airbus partner again in November 1978 with a 20% holding in the consortium and a £100m investment in the A310. BAe would continue to build the A300 wings and thereafter the wings for the A310.

Airbus A320 and further Airbus airliners

Henceforward BAe had to invest in each new Airbus project and in 1983 it was faced with investing heavily in the innovative 150-180 seater A320. While its two international partners were nationalised and could raise the funds comparatively easily, even raising the £250m required for the launch aid from the Thatcher Government for the wing was an effort.

BAe had already invested £350m of its own funds in the A300 and A310. Substantial investment from the Government and BAe followed in 1987 for the A330/A340 programme and in 2000 for the A380.

Executive development BAe 125-800

The successful 125 executive jet had been developed by Hawker Siddeley since 1962 and remained in production thanks to constant refinements to keep it abreast of the competition.

The BAe Board agreed to invest in its next development, the 125-800, to maintain its market share. The 125-800 version not only had uprated engines, but underwent a substantial redesign, to improve its performance and spaciousness, plus its looks, an important feature in the executive market.

ATP

In addition to the launch of the A320 in 1984, British Aerospace went ahead with its long-awaited BAe 748 replacement, the ATP (Advanced TurboProp) assembled at Woodford. There were high expectations that the ATP, as a second-generation, twin-turboprop airliner would emulate the 748's strong sales performance. This new project completed BAe's 'family' of civil aircraft, with Airbus offering all the large airliners, to take BAe into the 21st Century.

▲ BAe ATP G-MATP during its maiden flight from Woodford on 6 August 1986. *(BAE SYSTEMS)*

British Aerospace's military strategy

BAe's military business grew substantially in the 1980s - Tornado, Harrier and Hawk were all in production and winning export orders and the Nimrod AEW3 was being built at Woodford. Despite this positive situation, the company clearly needed successors to fill its factories. When BAC and Hawker Siddeley were merged into BAe in 1977 there were two military aircraft centres, BAC's at Warton and HSA's at Kingston and it was the former BAC plant which gradually became the hub within BAe.

Tornado

Whereas the UK component of the tripartite Tornado bomber's design, testing and production planning had been BAC's responsibility, BAe now had the advantage of projected orders for over 800 aircraft, providing employment for 70,000 people in the UK, Germany and Italy.

EAP and Eurofighter

In the late 1970s, British, French, German, and Italian companies had initiated discussions aimed at collaboratively designing, developing, and producing

British Aerospace's military aircraft and missiles on display at Warton. A Typhoon leading, then behind a Harrier GR5 (left) and Sea Harrier FA2 (right). The next row has a Hawk 200 (left) and Hawk 100 ZA101 (right), at the back are two Tornado F3s either side of a Tornado GR1. In between these are Sky Flash, Sea Wolf, Sea Skua and Martell missiles. Rapier missile mobile launchers are also there, as is a Swingfire mobile launcher at the rear on the right. *(BAE SYSTEMS via Warton Heritage)*

Three of the seven Eurofighter development aircraft: German DA1 98+29, British DA2 ZH588 and DA4 ZH590. DA1 and DA2 flew in 1994 and DA4 in 1997.
(BAE SYSTEMS via Warton Heritage)

Inset: BAE SYSTEMS logo from 1999.

BAE SYSTEMS

Europe's next generation fighter aircraft. These talks foundered in 1981 when no commonality could be found among the respective air forces.

Eager to not be stymied by Government inaction, BAe and UK ancillary industry partners lobbied the Government in early 1983 to produce a 'proof of concept' technology demonstrator. It would be an unstable, 'fly by wire' aircraft constructed in part from composites and would employ elements of stealth. The Government agreed to part-fund it in May 1983. The EAP (Experimental Aircraft Programme) flew in August 1986 and proved a great success.

EAP's success led the way to Eurofighter a collaborative venture with Germany, Italy and Spain. Though the project was broadly agreed in 1988 and prototypes started flying in 1994, actual production contracts were only placed in 1998 owing to Germany's reluctance to commit to the budget.

Harriers and Hawks
By 1977 the Harrier was in operation with the RAF and the US Marines and production of the FRS1 was well in hand UK's Royal Navy at Kingston and Dunsfold. The first FRS1 flew in August 1978 so sufficient numbers were available for the Navy's aircraft carriers during the war against the Argentines to regain the Falkland Islands during 1982. Following the clear success of the RN's Harriers in

the South Atlantic, 60 of the developed Harrier FRS2s were ordered.

Surprisingly the next major Harrier development was led by McDonnell Douglas with BAe as a major sub-contractor. The original BAe-McDonnell Douglas collaboration had ended and each had designed differing developments of the aircraft. As the US forces orders for the McDonnell Douglas version were far greater than the RAF's 60, the UK accepted this much cheaper version.

The Hawk which had made its maiden flight in 1974, just three years prior to BAe's formation, was being delivered to the RAF and was selling well abroad. The improved version of the twin-seater, the Hawk 100 with a combat wing was launched in 1982 and in a move to expand BAe's portfolio of military aircraft even further, a single-seat version, the Hawk 200 which flew in 1986 was devised for air forces needing an inexpensive attack aircraft.

Al Yamamah contract
Building on the contract that BAC won in 1965 from Saudi Arabia for Lightnings and Strikemasters, BAe won its biggest-ever arms export deal in September 1985, to supply 132 aircraft to Saudi Arabia in a contract estimated to be worth up to £4bn. The contract was for 48 Tornado GR1s, 24 Tornado F3s, 30 Hawks, Rapier missiles and 48 Swiss-built Pilatus PC-9

turboprop training aircraft. This agreement cemented the relationship between BAe and Saudi Arabia, which is one of the company's current major markets. These orders guaranteed work for years ahead, along with training and spares.

BAe's widens its reach – takeovers of Royal Ordnance, Rover Group and more
In April 1987 BAe purchased all 15 factories of Royal Ordnance, the UK munitions provider. With this purchase, BAe became the majority supplier of munitions to the UK forces, marking a strategic move towards redefining itself as a defence company and not only an aerospace manufacturer. It had also purchased an electronics and communications company, Sperry Gyroscope, a construction company, Ballast Needham and Arlington Securities to manage the sale of its redundant sites.

The stock market was surprised in March 1987 when the purchase of state-owned, loss-making British volume car manufacturer, Rover Group (previously British Leyland) was announced. The Chairman of BAe, Roland Smith announced, "This will be the biggest manufacturing business in Britain, that is a position of considerable power..." Smith's philosophy was to emulate Germany's Daimler-Benz, a car, aerospace and defence giant.

BAe flies into turbulence and looks for partners

In September 1991, British Aerospace's profits slumped and the company had to increase the pace of rationalisation and restructuring of its businesses in the face of constrained UK defence spending, brought about by the end of the Cold War. BAe began considering possible disposals or partners for its core businesses. During 1992 matters with Regional Aircraft worsened, as many of BAe's airliners were returned off lease at reduced values. The Rover Group's cars were also doing extremely badly but there were strong, growing sales from Airbus.

The following year matters worsened, there were substantial redundancies, the closure of Hatfield and the sale of the Hamble factory, but the share price continued to decline. The real problem was with the Regional Aircraft Division with its large losses. BAe came close to ruin as it was hit by this financial crisis brought on by the potential financial exposure to its regional aircraft lease book. There were concerns that the company might collapse, even though many of its products were on a firm footing with plenty of orders, for example, Tornado, (which received a repeat order from Saudi Arabia in late 1992), Hawk, Harrier and the Sea Eagle missile.

The company flies into calmer air

BAe's Corporate Jets Division which produced the 125 executive jet range was making many sales so as part of the programme to improve BAe's finances, it was sold to Raytheon for £250 million in mid-1993.

Considering that after its many troubles, BAe was only valued at £1bn, the sale of the 125 Programme for a quarter of this amount was a great benefit

BAe Nimrod MRA4 development aircraft PA2 ZJ518 which made its maiden flight from Woodford to Warton on 12 December 2004. (BAE SYSTEMS via Warton Heritage)

▼ **HMS Artful under construction at BAE's factory at Barrow-in-Furness. It is the third member of the Astute class and is a 300ft long, 7,400 ton, nuclear-powered, Hunter-Killer submarine. It carries torpedoes and Tomahawk missiles.** *(BAE SYSTEMS)*

to the firm. Some felt it was a shame for BAe to sell its only clearly profitable civil programme.

At the beginning of 1994, BAe disposed of Rover Group, the troublesome car manufacturer it had bought in 1988 and sold it to German volume car maker BMW for £800m. Another disposal was BAe Space Systems which was sold to Matra Marconi Space in 1996. With these disposals and the closure of sites the company was now on a sound financial footing.

BAe's civil airliner closures

Though the company had now resolved many of its immediate financial problems, the ATP, which was the company's 748 replacement, had made little headway in the market and was being outsold by the Franco-Italian ATR42 and ATR72. From the beginning of 1993, the loss-making ATP was transferred to Prestwick and it was renamed the Jetstream 61 as part of the Jetstream family along with the Jetstream 31 and 41 that were already in production there. In this way, all turboprop airliner production was at a single site. This move tidied up BAe's turboprop range and was designed to make them more attractive to a partner. This transfer did little for the rebranded Jetstream 61 and when BAe joined a pan-European regional aircraft consortium - Aero International (Regional), the Jetstream 61 was in direct competition with the ATR family and production ended in 1995.

Production of the 19-seat J31 had already effectively ground to a halt, leaving Prestwick with only the J41. Orders for the Jetstream 41 the 30-seater successor to the Jetstream 31, had proved very erratic and finding that it could only sell aircraft at a loss the company ended production, withdrawing entirely from the turboprop airliner market in 1997. Besides its very profitable 20% holding in Airbus, for which BAe built 187 wing sets in 1997, its portfolio of civil aircraft was now reduced to just the 146, by now renamed the RJ (Regional Jet), which delivered 22 aircraft from Woodford in the same year.

Space Systems

Just to illustrate the whirligig that company acquisitions and disposals can create. In 1994 British Aerospace Space Systems was sold to Matra Marconi Space. Yet in 1999 BAe regained an interest in the company when it merged with GEC's Marconi Electronic Systems to form BAE SYSTEMS. In 2000, Matra Marconi was merged with the space division of DaimlerChrysler Aerospace (DASA) to form Astrium. BAE sold its 25% stake in June 2003 and the company became EADS Astrium and in 2013 Airbus Space and Defence.

Military developments – Typhoon enters production

In 1995 British Aerospace signed an agreement with Saab to form Saab-BAe Gripen AB which lasted for 15 years. It was a joint marketing, support and manufacturing agreement for an export variant of the Saab JAS39 Gripen.

Even though BAe's factories lost much of their civil aircraft work in the mid-1990s these losses were leavened in July 1996 when BAe won the contract to replace the Nimrod MR2 with the MRA4. When production of the Harrier and Tornado ended in 1998, there were upgrade programmes on them at Warton, along with Typhoon, which had finally entered production.

More mergers - Matra-BAe Dynamics - MBDA

In 1996 BAe and Matra missiles formed Matra-BAe Dynamics and this became the largest missile manufacturer in Europe with the aim of matching US missile makers, Hughes and Raytheon. This was but the first step in a major realignment of BAe's Dynamics Division. It later merged with EADS, GEC and Alenia to form MBDA. BAE Systems and Airbus Space and Defence each have holdings of 37.5% and Leonardo 25%.

British Aerospace becomes BAE SYSTEMS

In the late 1990s BAe began merger talks with Daimler-Chrysler Aerospace (later DASA) with which they were already partners on the Tornado and Typhoon. This merger would have provided the merged grouping a 58% share of Airbus, putting the French into a minority position on the grouping. This merger came very close to fruition but at the last moment BAe bought

▲ BAE SYSTEMS Land (UK) manufactured the Challenger 2 tanks which serve with the British and Omani Army. The British Army's Challengers will shortly undergo a Life Extension Programme.
(BAE SYSTEMS)

British-based GEC-Marconi. Attempts to make a tripartite tie up of BAe, GEC-Marconi and DASA failed as DASA only wanted a bilateral merger. BAe's action drove DASA into the arms of Aérospatiale-Matra of France and CASA of Spain to form EADS a year later – the third largest defence supplier in the world after Lockheed Martin and Boeing.

On completion of its merger BAe renamed itself BAE SYSTEMS to reflect more accurately the new company's portfolio. In taking over GEC-Marconi the shipbuilder VSEL at Barrow became part of its portfolio and it also gained a foothold in the USA.

BAE ends British-built airliner production

On 21 March 2000 BAE SYSTEMS, had launched the Avro RJX, a limited re-engined development of the RJ. BAE would only invest heavily in new civil major projects with Airbus - that was the product to invest in, take the risk and get the return. The first flight of the

Avro RJX85 prototype took place in April 2001 and it was soon joined by a second aircraft but on 27 November 2001, BAE stated that due to a downturn in the market following 9/11 the Regional Jet business was no longer viable and so production of the RJ ended and the RJX was cancelled. This reduced BAE's civil airliner business to just profitable Airbus.

New Aircraft Carrier contract

In February 2003 BAE won a contract to share the production of the Navy's two mighty new aircraft carriers with the French multinational Thales, but with the work to be carried out entirely in British shipyards. These would be the largest British warships ever built and were designed to carry 40 offensive aircraft including helicopters. BAE's relationship with the MoD was at a low ebb at the time owing to both the new 'Astute' class nuclear submarine and Nimrod MRA4 contracts being much over budget and behind schedule.

However by 2009 BAE had secured a

The first two Eurofighter Typhoons delivered to the Royal Saudi Air Force, registered as 1001 and 1002. They are still carrying UK military serials ZK060 and ZK061. *(BAE SYSTEMS)*

monopoly in warship manufacture in the domestic market with the takeover of VT Group.

BAE takes over UK and US military vehicle manufacturers

In March 2005 BAE SYSTEMS planted its flag firmly at the centre of the US defence market by a takeover of United Defense Industries, manufacturer of Bradley armoured fighting vehicles. This was BAE's biggest takeover since its 1999 merger of the old British Aerospace with GEC's Marconi defence businesses. It also meant that that the US Department of Defense, not Britain's Ministry of Defence, would become the company's largest customer. Clearly this was part of BAE's strategy of becoming a transatlantic defence and aerospace contractor.

UDI was best-known for its Bradley fighting vehicles, for howitzers and for providing all the guns for the US Navy. BAE's existing armoured vehicles business in the UK, centred on Challenger tank manufacturer Alvis Vickers, which BAE had taken over in 2004, was now subsumed into BAE's enlarged Land Systems business, with headquarters in Arlington County, Virginia near Washington D.C. The takeover of Alvis had also provided BAE with a monopoly of UK military vehicle manufacture.

In a continuation of its strategy to expand its holdings in the US, BAE expanded its US holdings two years later with the acquisition of Armor Holdings, US maker of military vehicles and body armour. With this purchase, BAE further strengthened its position in the USA, a market from which it was already making 40% of its total sales.

BAE sells its holding in Airbus

After cancellation of the Avro RJX in 2001, BAE's only civil programme was Airbus wing production at Broughton and Filton. With the formation of EADS in 2000 when Aerospatiale, Deutsche Airbus and CASA all merged, BAE was left out in the cold at Airbus with just a 20% stake in it. Not a happy position for a large player like BAE and in September 2006 when Airbus was having problems with the A380, BAE sold its share for £1.87bn. This marked BAE's final disengagement from civil aircraft manufacture.

More Saudi sales

A contract for 72 Eurofighter Typhoon multi-role fighters assembled at Warton was signed in August 2006. BAE stated that it had earned £43 billion in twenty years from Saudi contracts and that it could earn £40 billion more. It is Britain's largest ever export agreement, and employs upwards of 5,000 people in Saudi Arabia.

BAE SYSTEMS Australia becomes that country's largest defence contractor

Just as BAE was expanding operations in the USA, at the beginning of 2008 BAE consolidated its position in Australia to became the country's largest defence contractor.

Cyber security

The company's strategy has not only been to expand into traditional forms of defence but also to invest in Cyber security and it made several purchases to strengthen and develop its position. It aims to help nations, governments and

▲ Typhoon FGR4 ZK358 and the sole Taranis ZZ250 at Warton. In July 2010 BAE unveiled its low-observable UCAV technology demonstrator, Taranis to the aviation media at Warton. Taranis is a UK-only technology demonstrator, with BAE Systems heading a joint MoD/industry team. *(BAE SYSTEMS)*

businesses to defend themselves against cybercrime, reduce their risk in this connected world, comply with regulation and transform their operations.

UK Defence cuts 2010 – Harrier and Nimrod axed

In 2010 there was change of Government in the UK and the new administration carried out some huge cuts to the armed forces. The Nimrod MRA4 which was about to enter service was cancelled and all the airframes scrapped, the Harrier force was grounded and sold off as spares to the US Marines. Owing to the loss of Harrier work at Warton, Hawk final assembly was relocated from Brough to Warton.

BAE SYSTEMS now

The company continues to look to develop its position in the world. In 2012 detailed talks took place about linking up with EADS which would have been a grand British – French – German – Spanish Aerospace and Defence grouping but political opposition in Germany was rumoured to have been the problem with progressing this further.

BAE SYSTEMS has similarities with that famous British company, Vickers-Armstrongs which was an armaments, tank, warship and aircraft manufacturer, which exported its products all over the world. BAE is the prime contractor of all the UK's major defence projects; Typhoon, F-35, Hawk, the Astute class and successor nuclear submarines, the two aircraft carriers, the Type 26 frigates and armoured fighting vehicles and is the world's third largest defence contractor. ∎

Legacy aircraft programmes

Legacy Aircraft

When British Aerospace took over BAC and Hawker Siddeley in 1977 it inherited refurbishment programmes on aircraft out of production and work on aircraft very near the end of their production cycle. The amount of work carried out on these aircraft was substantial and illustrates the extent to which the manufacturer's connection with an aircraft may continue for many years after the last one has left the production line.

Military aircraft
■ Canberra

The first English Electric Canberra VN799, flew in May 1949 and proved a remarkably profitable investment for the manufacturers and their successors including BAe. Owing to the Cold War and the threat of nuclear war, large orders were placed with English Electric and other manufacturers. Many versions were developed, most notably for reconnaissance as the Canberra had remarkable altitude performance. The Canberra had many roles in the RAF and the last examples of the aircraft to remain in service were photo-reconnaissance PR9s which were retired late as 2006.

A grand total of 1,376 Canberras were built (including licence-built) of which 782 served with the RAF. Twenty-one different versions were operated by twenty-one countries. 115 ex-RAF aircraft were rebuilt and exported, in addition to 143 newly built export aircraft. The final delivery of a newly-built Canberra was to South African Air Force in February 1964. However large numbers returned to the factory for maintenance, refurbishment and modification at Samlesbury for new roles as new marks by the RAF and as testbeds. This was also the case with overseas operators of the Canberra who frequently returned theirs. In fact, owing to the continued demand for Canberras in the 1960s, BAC purchased large numbers of RAF aircraft that were surplus to requirements. The refurbishment work at the Samlesbury factory provided BAC/BAe with an excellent income stream throughout the 1960s, 1970s and right up until 1988.

■ Lightning

The Lightning was the only all-British supersonic fighter aircraft to enter production. It evolved from the P1A research aircraft which flew in August 1954 to become a superlative interceptor aircraft for the RAF and took on an attack role with the Royal Saudi Air Force and the Kuwaiti Air Force. Development took the aircraft from the F1 to the F3, T4, T5 and F6 with the RAF. The export versions were the F53 and the T55.

The last Lightning built left BAC Warton on delivery to Saudi Arabia on 4 September 1972, but this was not the end of Warton's connection with the type. By late 1970 the number of Lightnings in RAF service had reached a peak of approximately 150, equipping nine front-line squadrons and a large Operational Conversion Unit.

During the 1970s, the RAF Lightning fighter squadrons were gradually disbanded. The rundown programme was then suspended when the RAF realized that it was about to have a shortage of fighter aircraft as the Tornado F2 would be entering service later than planned. With greater demands put on the Lightnings, fatigue was likely to become an issue. To prolong their lives, a wing root strengthening programme was instigated and in 1985 some thirty-five F6s were returned to what was now British Aerospace Warton, to extend their

Lightning F6 XP693 and Tornado F3 ZE785. XP693 first flew in June 1962 was retained by BAC/BAe for development work at Warton until 1992. Its final task was as a chase aircraft on the Tornado programme. The Tornados replaced the Lightnings in RAF service. *(BAE SYSTEMS via Warton Heritage)*

lives by another 400 hours. In 1987 the Lightning Training Flight and No 5 Squadron were disbanded leaving just No 11 Squadron active at RAF Binbrook until 30 April 1988 when the unit was re-equipped with the Tornado F3, (built at the same Samlesbury and Warton factories as the Lightnings).

■ Strikemaster

The Jet Provost was a jet-powered basic trainer providing side-by-side seating for the instructor and student pilot. The early marks of the aircraft were development machines and the RAF received 386 Jet Provost T3s and T4s between June 1959 and 1965. Following Luton's closure, development passed to Warton where the pressurised T5s were built.

Recognising the potential of the T5, BAC offered an inexpensive weapons trainer or counter-insurgency version: the Strikemaster. It had four pylons for bombs or rocket launchers, giving a total weapon load of 3,000lb including two guns. The aircraft was cleared to 6g at an all-up

▲ Vulcan K2 XM571 following its conversion by BAe Woodford from a B2 to a K2 tanker. *(Avro Heritage)*

weight of 11,500lb and was capable of taking the student pilot right through to combat. The largest customer was the RSAF which received forty-seven Mk 80s.

The delivery of the 146th Strikemaster took place at Warton in 1978 with a delivery to the Royal Saudi Air Force. BAe built ten Strikemasters for stock of which three were sold to Sudan, one to Oman, and six to Ecuador, with the final delivery in October 1988. In the meantime the Kuwait Air Force traded back its nine remaining Strikemasters to British Aerospace and these were refurbished and sold to the Botswana Defence Force in 1987 which maintained them in service until 1997.

■ Vulcan

The mighty Vulcan was the last of the RAF's three 'V' bombers to maintain its bombing role but as it was about to be withdrawn from service was called into action in the Falklands War.

The Vulcan had made its first flight on 30 August 1952 and deliveries of the Vulcan B1s to the RAF began in 1955, but plans were afoot to further develop it and improve all areas of its operating envelope so by 1967 all the Vulcan units had the superior performing B2s. As there

Royal Saudi Air Force Strikemaster 1120. *(BAE SYSTEMS via Warton Heritage)*

Low pass over the hangars at Holme-on-Spalding-Moor by Buccaneer S2 XV358. *(BAE SYSTEMS)*

was little likelihood by the late 1950s that the RAF's 'V' bombers could successfully fly deep over enemy territory without interception, Vulcans and Victors were armed with the Blue Steel strategic nuclear missile. Blue Steel was never used in anger and with the introduction of the Navy's Polaris nuclear missile the RAF lost its nuclear deterrent role but 60 Vulcans were maintained in service as strategic bombers and were due to be replaced by Tornados during 1982.

Black Buck – the longest bombing mission in history

When Argentina invaded the Falklands Islands on 2 April 1982 there was no expectation of bombing missions by land-based units as the nearest friendly landfall was on Asencion Island, more than 4,500 miles from the Falklands. However Asencion was suitable as a staging post for the task force and had a USAF base at Wideawake Airfield with a long runway. At RAF Waddington, five Vulcans with Olympus 301s and wing pylon attachments had their flight refuelling systems reactivated and were readied for a conventional bombing mission. New inertial navigation systems were trialled and integrated while in-flight refuelling was hurriedly practiced with Victors. A radar jamming pod was mounted on one of the underwing pylons.

On 30 April a huge operation ensued to get one Vulcan to be able drop 21 1,000lb bombs on Port Stanley airfield. A total of eleven Victors had to refuel each other and the Vulcan to get it to the target. Descending to just 250ft for the bombing run the Vulcan XM607 dropped bombs over Port Stanley airfield, quickly

⌃ **Aircraft packed in the hangars at BAe Brough in 1987. Two RAF Phantoms in the background, a Jetstream and two of the 48 Pilatus PC-9s ordered for the RSAF. BAe had promoted the PC-9 for the RAF but despite the service's preference for the PC-9, the Tucano was ordered and built at Shorts. If the PC-9 had been selected for the RAF the PC-9s would have been assembled at Brough. The RSAF PC-9s were built by Pilatus at Stans in Switzerland, flown to Brough for completion to the customer's specification and delivery.** *(BAE SYSTEMS)*

climbed away and set course for Wideawake. Short of fuel it fortunately rendezvoused with a Victor and returned safely.

The results of the raid were satisfactory, though the runway was still usable by Hercules and lighter aircraft. Of the six further 'Black Bucks' planned, two were aborted and the other five were bombing or anti-radar attacks.

The Vulcan's final role

Once the Falkland Islands had been liberated there seemed little further need for the Vulcans despite their valiant deeds. However as the Victor K2s had been over-worked during 'Operation Corporate' there was an urgent need for more tanker capacity. Nine VC10 tankers were being converted at Filton but additional aerial tanking capacity was paramount and it was decided that the Vulcan would fit the bill. So much so that after initial discussions on 30 April, the go-ahead was given just a few days later on 4 May 1982.

When installation in the bomb bay was found to be unsuitable, it was decided to install a Hose Drum Unit (HDU) in the rear ECM bay. As the bomb bay was not used, a third bomb bay fuel tank could also be fitted giving the Vulcan an overall fuel capacity of 100,000lbs. Six Vulcans were converted at BAe Woodford (where they had been built) and flew with No.50 Squadron until the end of March 1984 when they were replaced by newly-rebuilt VC10 tankers.

The Buccaneer

In answer to the Royal Navy requirement for a high subsonic speed, twin-seat, twin-jet, carrier strike aircraft able to deliver nuclear or conventional weapons in all weathers, Blackburn devised the Buccaneer. The prototype XK486 made its maiden flight on 30 April 1958 and by the end of 1961 all the 20 development aircraft were airborne. It had an obvious capability as a land-based tactical strike aircraft, and the manufacturers made many presentations to both for the RAF and foreign governments, to win just one export order - in October 1962 the South African Air Force placed an order for 16.

The first operational RN squadron, equipped with the Buccaneer S1, No. 801 Squadron was commissioned in July 1962 and others soon followed. However the Gyron-engined S1 was under-powered so the Rolls-Royce Spey-

powered Buccaneer S2 was developed. The Navy found the greater power and equipment refinements provided a far superior aircraft and by the end of the 1960s the S1s had all been retired from active service.

After the Government cancelled the F-111, in July 1968 the MoD announced as an 'interim measure' that the RAF would now inherit sixty-four Buccaneers from the Fleet Air Arm made redundant by the scrapping of the aircraft carrier fleet along with twenty-six newly-built aircraft. This 'interim measure' continued until 1994 when the Buccaneer was replaced by the Tornado.

With the RAF

In parallel with this new production, a refurbishment programme at Brough converted some 64 ex-Royal Navy Buccaneer S2As to RAF standards. The initial batch of these refurbished aircraft was delivered to the RAF in October 1969 and the first new S2B flew in January 1970. Further orders kept the Brough production line busy to the end of 1977, by which time 209 had been built.

The majority of the ex-Royal Navy Buccaneers S2As transferred to the RAF were ultimately modified to full S2B standard with the ability to carry the Martel TV-guided air-to-surface missile and incorporating the bomb door fuel tank modification. This added another 425gals to the existing fuel capacity and gave a pronounced bulge on the Buccaneer's underbelly.

Buccaneers grounded and return to service

During a 'Red Flag' exercise at Nellis Air Force Base in Nevada in February 1980, a 15 Sqn Buccaneer crashed into the desert after its wing had broken off. All machines were immediately grounded. The cause of the additional stress to the airframe was primarily because of the wing tip fairing extension fitted to the S2s. Two Buccaneers with the greatest flying hours were totally dismantled at BAe Brough and examined minutely and one of the pair was tested to destruction. The repair was very complicated, requiring a dismantling of the aircraft down to its basic structure and either the shaving of 0.1inches from a metal rib to remove the crack in the structure or the total removal and replacement of the front spar.

All the aircraft were assessed, some did not need modification, some did and some were scrapped. All bar two of the aircraft in Nevada flew home and the remaining two were shipped home for repair. To maintain the crews' flying hours, a fleet of 34 Hunters was assembled so they could keep flying. After six months, Buccaneer flying was gradually resumed.

By 1983 with the introduction of the Tornado into service the Buccaneers' roles were reduced to maritime strike and reconnaissance and all the squadrons were based at Lossiemouth. It was recognised that their weapons suite was insufficient, so 42 aircraft were earmarked for modification to carry the BAe Dynamics Sea Eagle and host of other improvements to keep the aircraft viable ➤

▼ First VC10 K2 tanker ZA141 taking off on its maiden flight from Filton on 22 June 1982. This aircraft was formerly G-ARVG with British Airways and Gulf Air.
(BAE SYSTEMS)

into the 1990s. As Brough was fully occupied with Harrier and Hawk work, the aircraft were flown into BAe Woodford and were converted there by workers from Brough.

Gulf War and finale

Following Iraq's invasion of Kuwait in 1990 the when the RAF Tornados were needed to attack infrastructure in Iraq there was a problem as the TIALD *(Thermal Imaging Airborne Laser Designator)* targeting pod which illuminated the target was still under development. At short notice, twelve Buccaneers of Nos 12 and 208 Sqn were deployed to support the Tornados with their Paveway system and Laser guided bombs. Additionally they carried ECM (Electronic Counter-Measures) pods and as a first received defensive weaponry in the form of one Sidewinder missile. 212 sorties were flown and the aircraft returned to the UK in desert pink camouflage and with their 'gung ho' markings. Over the remaining years of their service their popularity grew but on 31 March 1994 they were withdrawn from service.

Not only Buccaneers but also Phantoms

As the BAe Brough factory was the Sister Design Company for the UK's US-built

▲ VC10 K4 ZD242 and two Tornado F3s over the Falkland Islands. This Super VC10 was formerly G-ASGP with British Airways, it spent nine years parked at Abingdon before it was flown to Filton for tanker conversion work to begin. (Paul Morris)

Phantoms, it carried out major structural repair on them. During their UK service with the RN and the RAF from 1968 to 1991, many Phantoms returned to Brough for repairs to the airframe owing to fatigue problems and four machines had their centre wings replaced. The Phantoms typically had repairs to their wing fold ribs, main spars and four of the aircraft even received replacement wings.

Vickers VC10 – BAe's tanker rebuilds

Even though production of the long-range VC10 airliner had ended in 1970 with the completion of the 54th aircraft, the manufacturer's involvement was far from over and BAe was to carry out substantial work on them.

The RAF had originally ordered 14 VC10 C1s for use in a trooping/cargo role. One of these became the RB211 test bed with Rolls-Royce and was wastefully scrapped on completion of these trials. These RAF aircraft had provision for refuelling in flight but were not flight refuelling tankers, although later modified to take on this role.

In April 1978, British Aerospace began work at Filton on the conversion of nine VC10s into tankers. These came in two distinct groups; four formerly East African Airways Super VC10s repossessed by BAe

in 1977 and five former British Airways Standard VC10s which had flown with Gulf Air for almost four years and been retired at the end of 1977.

From airliners to aerial tankers

The conversion was an extensive process. The aircraft were stripped down to the bare airframe. To have commonality with the VC10 C1s all the Tanker VC10s received Rolls-Royce Conway R.Co 43s and were fitted with an Artouste APU in the tail cone. Five fuselage fuel tanks were installed in each aircraft providing 13 tons of fuel. The Standard VC10 then had a total of 166,000lbs fuel with wing and cabin tanks while the Supers with their additional fin fuel tanks carried a total capacity of 181,000lbs fuel. Each aircraft had three refuelling points, two underwing pods and Hose Drum Unit fitted into the rear freight bay of the aircraft. The RAF designated the Standard VC10 tankers as VC10 K2 and the Supers as K3s.

The Tanker VC10 flight test programme and its difficulties

The first VC10 K2 tanker to fly was ZA141 which completed a 3½ hour first flight on 22 June 1982 captained by Roy Radford. This first K2 was painted in dark green and dark grey camouflage like the Victors it

Filton factory was ZA148 (ex-5Y-ADA) in July 1984 and 101 Squadron received it and the three other Super VC10 K3s in late 1984 and 1985.

More VC10 tankers

When British Airways retired their Super VC10s from airline service in 1981 the remaining fleet was bought by the Ministry of Defence. Three were delivered to Brize Norton and scrapped, with a further eleven delivered to RAF Abingdon and put into store. The Ministry intended to convert them to tankers but the decision was delayed several times. By 1987 with the MoD aware that the remaining Victors would soon be retired, British Aerospace was tasked with assessing which of the VC10s inactive at Abingdon for six years were too riddled with corrosion and which could be kept on. As a result five were scrapped that year, leaving just six, all of which were also suffering from serious corrosion.

The VC10 K4 and C1(K) conversion programme

In 1990 BAe and Flight Refuelling (FRA) won the contract to convert five of the former BA Supers to three-point tankers and the RAF's VC10 C1s were to become VC10 C1(K)s with underwing refuelling pods. BAe would convert the Supers into VC10 K4s and FRA the VC10 C1s. British Aerospace handling the flight trials of both the K4s and the C1(K)s. This would provide the RAF with a very flexible fleet; 13 tanker/transport VC10 C1(K)s and a total of 14 VC10 K2, K3 and K4 tankers.

Work began on bringing back to life the long dormant Super VC10s which

had remained at Abingdon for nine years. On 27 July 1990 ZD242 (ex-G-ASGP) was ferried to Filton. The other Super VC10s then left Abingdon for Filton at three-monthly intervals. The scale of the work to rebuild and modify the Supers into K4s was demonstrated by the three years that ZD242 spent at Filton until its first flight as a tanker on 29 July 1993 and the last ZD235 flying on 13 December 1995. The first K4 was delivered to No 101 Squadron in 1994 and by early 1996 it had 14 VC10 tankers on its strength. The K4s became three-point tankers like the others but differed significantly from the K3 as fuel tanks were not fitted in their fuselages. Even so they still carried 50 tons of disposable fuel to transfer. The fuselage tanks were not fitted as owing to the age of the aircraft it was felt best not to cut open the fuselage roof to fit them as was done on the K2. This provided greater operational flexibility as with the large passenger cabin still available for use, the K4s kept their cabin trim and were fitted with 35 seats.

In the meantime the No 10 Squadron VC10 C1s were gradually converted to VC10 C1(K)s by Flight Refuelling Aviation at Hurn. At Hurn they were fitted with underwing Mk32 refuelling pods and alterations the refuelling system. On completion they were then flown to Filton for flight testing by BAe. The first C1K XV101 was completed in June 1992 and the contract came to an end when XR808 flew in February 1997. As the VC10s were repainted their hemp or white and grey livery was replaced by an all grey livery.

was to replace but was repainted before delivery in hemp. The rest of the fleet were in hemp from the start.

On the 16th flight ZA141 piloted by Roy Radford was carrying out diving trials with air brakes out when he met with difficulties. The tailplane began to oscillate in an alarming manner and with increasing force. The VC10 was clearly in a dangerous situation and might lose its tail. Radford selected airbrakes in and the oscillation damped out but the aircraft continued to accelerate and during recovery from the dive the pilots had to pull back heavily on the controls, exceeding its diving speed. During post-flight examination, serious damage to the integral structure of the fin was discovered some of which had been caused by previous fatigue damage to the fin. ZA141's fin and tail were removed and replaced with those of RAE Bedford's VC10, XX914.

Handover of the first VC10 K2 to 101 Squadron

The third VC10 K2, ZA140 was the first to be handed over to the RAF at a ceremony at Filton on 25 July 1983 and flew its first operational sortie on 1 January 1984 during the deployment of RAF Jaguars to the USA to participate in Red Flag. The first Super VC10 tanker to appear from the

⌃ Although the General Dynamics F-111 was not a BAe legacy programme it provided substantial work for the firm. Between 1978 and 1992 BAe Filton worked on 328 UK-based F-111Es from 20TFW Upper Heyford and F-111Fs from 48TFW Lakenheath. *(BAE SYSTEMS)*

RAF VC10s in service

The RAF's original VC10 C1s of 10 Squadron played a major role in 'Operation Corporate' and two aircraft converted into full 'Casevac' role and others busy supporting operations. Subsequently despite all their other usual duties they now had to support the UK forces in the liberated Falklands. With the arrival of the VC10 tankers from 1984 the total VC10 fleet grew to 27 at its peak. They were active in support and tanker roles from the Falklands, over former Yugoslavia in the mid-1990s, airstrikes over Afghanistan after 9/11, where five VC10 tankers supported USN aircraft operating from carriers in the Indian Ocean. This operation was succeeded by 'Operation Herrick', the UK's operations in Afghanistan from 2002 which ended in 2014.

Despite ongoing operations in 2003, the emphasis temporarily shifted back to Iraq and 101 Squadron crews were heavily involved in the 'Operation Telic', the invasion and final overthrow of Saddam Hussein's regime. They would typically transfer 40 tons of fuel to RAF aircraft, USN F-18s, USAF, Italian or French types. Operations were not confined to refuelling, as 101 Squadron helped evacuate over 1,000 casualties to hospitals in Cyprus. Their last offensive operation was 'Operation Unified Protector', the liberation of Libya 2011 where they flew in support of RAF Tornados to enforce the 'no fly' zone and during hostilities which led to the downfall of Gaddafi.

With the VC10's numbers shrinking, by October 2005 there was a combined total of 17 airframes; ten C1(K), four K3s and three K4s so they were all concentrated into 101 Squadron. Numbers dwindled as aircraft were broken up for spares until the withdrawal of the VC10 from service in September 2013.

▲ Scottish Aviation Bulldog G-CBCB displaying its previous military serial XX537 at Fairford in July 2015. Scottish Aviation took over the project after the original manufacturer Beagle collapsed. *(Author)*

British Aerospace Filton's F-111 maintenance programme

In addition to its work on the VC10 Tanker conversion programme, between 1978 and 1992 BAe Filton worked on 328 UK-based F-111Es from 20TFW Upper Heyford and F-111Fs from 48TFW Lakenheath. The initial contract placed in September 1978, called for replacement of the pyrotechnics in the ejection capsule system. More contracts followed increasing the work to depot level maintenance. It was cheaper for the USAF to have the work done in the UK than returning the F-111s to USA for the work. By April 1984 Filton had worked on 100 USAF F-111s and the contract was extended again.

Owing to severe fatigue problems affecting the wing fold mechanism, it was decided that the structural integrity of the wing pivots and other prime structural components had to be thoroughly proof-tested at low temperatures. So a test facility was completed at Filton in mid-1986 to re-life the aircraft. The opening of this new test station negated the need for UK-based F-111s to return carried out to Sacramento, California. Many of the UK-based F-111s then passed through this facility at Filton.

Following the end of the Cold War, US forces in Europe were scaled back and the 14-year contract to service and re-lifing of the F-111 came to an end. The last F-111 left Filton on 16 September 1992.

Scottish Aviation and the Bulldog

The Bulldog had been developed by Beagle, the UK's last light aircraft manufacturer which went out of business in early 1970. It was a side-by-side, twin-seat 200hp Lycoming-engined primary trainer whose development trials had been part-completed at the time of Beagle's collapse.

Before it ceased trading Beagle had received an order for 58 aircraft (later raised to 78) from the Sweden. Scottish Aviation (SAL) speedily arranged to take over development and production to fulfil the Swedish order. SAL used the Beagle-converted prototype G-AXEH for

The roll out of the first licence-built ROMBAC One-Eleven 560 assembled at Banasea, Romania in August 1982. BAe supplied Romania with twenty-two aircraft sets of structural components, equipment, details and raw materials for the Romanian production line. Only nine were ever completed. *(BAE SYSTEMS)*

trials and the first production aircraft G-AYWN flew in June 1971. The Bulldog was also tested for a ground-support role and firing trials were completed with Sneb 68mm rockets from Matra launchers, while the Sweden Air Force Bulldogs were operational with the Bofors Bantam wire-guided missiles.

The Bulldog was chosen to replace the Chipmunk with the RAF which ordered 130 and production rate peaked at seven a month while this contract was being completed. Bulldog production ended in 1983 after 325 aircraft had been built with deliveries to ten customers, the largest of which were the RAF and Sweden.

Civil aircraft

BAe inherited three civil programmes from the former Hawker Siddeley. These were the twin turboprop 748, the 125 executive jet and the medium-range Trident jet airliner. The first and the second were established in production and had orders outstanding - the 125 clearly had great potential, and both aircraft were to receive further development. (See details of the 748 and 125 below.) In contrast production of the Trident at Hatfield was nearing its end with just ten Trident 2Es remaining on the production line for the CAAC, the Chinese State Airline.

From the former British Aircraft Corporation, BAe inherited the short-range One-Eleven jet airliner and Concorde. Production of the former was continuing at a low rate and there were proposals for major development which BAe would need to consider. As for Concorde, though it was rightly regarded as a great technical success it was then

clear by 1977 that no more than 16 production aircraft would be built, after the original expectation of sales of 150 aircraft.

The BAC One-Eleven after 1977 – developments that sadly came to nought

The BAC One-Eleven which first flew in August 1963 with 60 orders in hand seemed ready to emulate its turboprop predecessor, the Vickers Viscount, Britain's most successful airliner. Though there were major setbacks when the prototype crashed in a deep stall and there were two other accidents during the test programme, the One-Eleven entered service in April 1965.

The initial model, the One-Eleven 200 was developed into the 400 which had a greater payload, but despite requests from many airlines, it was not until September 1968 that the stretched 500 series entered service. A further development, the One-Eleven 475 which had the shorter fuselage of the 400 with the wings and higher-powered Speys of the 500 Series failed to make headway in the market. The Rolls-Royce Spey that powered the One-Eleven lacked growth potential and this held the aircraft back against the Douglas DC-9 and Boeing 737 and by the early 1970s, sales began to slow. By mid-1977 221 One-Elevens had been built by BAC and production was now at a very low level. (Only 14 more were delivered between then and the closure of the Hurn plant in 1984, when production was transferred to Romania.)

Licence production in Romania

With British Aerospace's decision to

⌃ N650DH, the first One-Eleven 400 re-engined with Rolls-Royce Tay engines during its maiden flight from San Antonio, Texas in July 1990.
(Bill Hurley)

develop the BAe 146 in 1978, further substantial development for the One-Eleven was at an end. The BAe Board entered into a licence production contract of the One-Eleven with Romania, the aircraft branded as ROMBAC One-Elevens, 'ROM' for Romania and 'BAC' for the original BAC.

The licensing agreement included the sale of three complete aircraft for the Romanian airline Tarom, to be built at Hum. But the main part of the deal was the supply of twenty-two aircraft sets of structural components, equipment, details and raw materials for the Romanian production line. After the twenty-second aircraft, indigenous One-Eleven production was to be established and the Romanian aircraft industry would be free to produce as many One-Elevens as it could sell. The three Hum-built aircraft comprised two 500s and a 475 freighter. The second 500, YR-BCO was ceremonially handed over on 12 March 1982 as the last One-Eleven to be completed at Hurn.

The production of One-Elevens at Baneasa in Romania, made painfully slow progress, and between 1982 and 1989, just nine ROMBAC One-Eleven 561RCs were produced leaving a two aircraft incomplete. With this slow rate of production ROMBAC was never a reliable supplier of aircraft and the nine aircraft were all initially delivered to Tarom but later leased to other operators.

The Tay One-Eleven

With the advent of the Rolls-Royce Tay engines in 1982, BAe Weybridge received enquiries from Corporate 400 series owners about the possibility of re-

engining the One-Elevens with the new engine. Using the Tay 650 with its powerful 15,100lb thrust, take-off performance would be increased by 32%, range by 500 miles and engine maintenance costs cut by up to 40%. With freight bay fuel tanks a Tay One-Eleven would have a transatlantic capability.

In July 1983 BAe Weybridge offered a programme of re-engining both 400 and 500 series aircraft to existing operators on the basis of thirty-five conversions. There was hope that one or other of the large operators would express an interest in re-engining their fleet, but none was forthcoming and the proposal was withdrawn.

Dee Howard and the Tay One-Eleven

The withdrawal of this BAe proposal really spelt the beginning of the end for the Tay One-Eleven project, for without the whole-hearted involvement of the manufacturer there was unlikely to be a viable programme. But Dee Howard of San Antonio went ahead with it. BAe and Rolls-Royce entered into an agreement with Dee Howard to provide expertise and technical data. Dee Howard assessed there appeared a good case for the re-engining, especially as the One-Eleven 500 series could outperform the BAe 146-300 and was probably equal to the Fokker 100.

The First Flight of the Tay One-Eleven

On Monday 2 July 1990, the Tay One-Eleven N650DH, marketed as the BAC 1-11 2400 made its first flight and was demonstrated at the Farnborough Air Show where it made a positive impression. Substantial progress had been made in the flight testing. John Lewis (BAe Chief Test Pilot, Filton) who captained the aircraft on her first flight and had led the test programme said that it was a superior machine to the 146. But on 17 November the first aircraft made its last flight and the second Tay One-Eleven N333GB flew a mere ninety-seven hours and was then grounded as Dee Howard had cancelled the project.

Romania and the Tay

Romaero met BAe, Rolls-Royce and Dee Howard in September 1991 and proposals were made to use YR-BRI and refit it with Tays. There were many difficulties to overcome; the lack of finance, BAe's lack of confidence in the Romanians and Rolls-Royce's desire to be supplier not an investor.

Too late, TAROM, the Romanian airline, announced they wanted to re-engine their One-Eleven fleet and Dee Howard offered the second Tay One-Eleven to Romaero who were unable to afford it. But these actions were pre-empted on 7 July 1993 when BAe withdrew from the Romaero operation entirely, apparently because of money owed by the Romanians. Licence production then ceased.

The One-Eleven continued in service in Europe in April 2002 when services were curtailed by new noise legislation. Aircraft migrated to other countries but soon faded from use. However, one aircraft remains in use as an F-35 radar testbed with Northrop Grumman in the USA.

Concorde – supersonic triumph

From 1977 until 2003, we could fly in comfort supersonically from London or Paris to New York in a little over three hours. This was an immense Anglo-French technological achievement created by BAC and Aerospatiale. The first two prototypes, F-WTSS and G-BSST flew in 1969 and engaged on a lengthy six-year test programme along with four other development aircraft.

The World's first supersonic passenger services

The first services began with simultaneous departures from London and Paris at 11:40 GMT on 21 January, 1976, with British Airways' G-BOAA flying non-stop to Bahrain and Air France's F-BVFA with a route from Paris to Rio de Janeiro via Dakar. These rather unexpected destinations were chosen as initially Concorde was unable to fly into

made profits in later years. Though each had small fleets they were clearly the airline's flagships.

The crash of F-BTSC at Paris-Charles de Gaulle on 25 July 2000 resulted in the aircraft being taken out of service. The cause of the accident was when a piece of debris left by a previous departing airliner cut open one of the Concorde's tyres sending large pieces of tyre into the underside of the wing penetrating the fuel tanks which then ignited.

Though BAe had originally inherited Design authority for Concorde from BAC, owing to the small size of the total fleet, Airbus oversaw this role for both the BA and Air France aircraft.

After modifications, Concorde returned to service sixteen months following the crash, but in the aftermath of 9/11 neither airline was making a profit with its services and in April 2003 both British Airways and Air France announced they would retire their Concordes. Air France ended operations on 24 May but British Airways organised a superb and very profitable long farewell of flights - keeping their fleet in revenue service until a grand finale at Heathrow on 24 October 2003.

The final day
On 24 October 2003, G-BOAG left from New York while two others made round trips, G-BOAF over the Bay of Biscay, carrying VIP guests including many former Concorde pilots, and G-BOAE visited Edinburgh making a supersonic dash up the North Sea. British Airways 'stole the show' by celebrating the end of Concorde operations with three aircraft landing in quick succession at Heathrow in front of huge crowds. The two round-trip Concordes landed at 16:01 and 16:03 followed at 16:05 pm by New York service.

That was the end of the era of supersonic passenger travel and twenty-seven years distinguished reign as BA's flagship. ■

the United States thanks to vehement protests from the environmental lobby.

Regular services from both London and Paris to Washington Dulles airport began on 24 May 1976. The American public's actual experience of Concorde proved that it was less noisy than people's expectations - noisier than a 707 on take-off but quieter on landing, and acceptance quickly grew. Gaining admittance to the more profitable and premier destination of JFK, New York, took another eighteen months, owing to the concerted opposition of pressure groups. Once Concorde gained access to New York it became its premier destination.

Disappointingly in September 1979 attempts to sell the remaining five unsold Concordes from the 16 production aircraft authorised by the British and French Governments were abandoned. BA then had a fleet of five and Air France four Concordes. Eventually BA took the two unsold British-built examples and Air France, the three unsold French ones. If production had been authorised beyond the 16 production aircraft, Concordes from number 17 onwards would have possessed substantially better performance. This improved performance would have been produced by an extended full-span droop wing leading edge, extended wing tips, increased fuel tankage and appreciable engine improvements which would have provided; quieter take offs, greater range

– enabling e.g. Frankfurt – New York non-stop.

Service and premature retirement
As the aircraft settled into service, they initially made a loss for both airlines. But more innovative marketing and many specialised charters, lead to large profits for British Airways' Concorde operation. Air France eventually followed suit and

▼ **Concorde G-BOAF landing at the 1988 Farnborough Air Show.**
(Derek Ferguson)

The 748 and its successor – the ATP

The prototype 748, G-APZV had made its maiden flight on 24 June 1960 and was joined by the second prototype G-ARAY on 10 April 1961. In July 1961 'RAY was upgraded to a 748 Series 2 when it was fitted with higher-powered Dart 531s which enabled it to fly at higher weights and at higher altitudes - which translated into either greater payload and/or longer range.

The licence-built Indian 748s
In July 1959 the Indian Government signed a contract with Hawker Siddeley for a licence to manufacture the 748 for the Indian Air Force. This was the biggest export order ever placed for a British aircraft still on the drawing board. Hindustan Aeronautics would manufacture the 748s in a newly-built factory at Kanpur.

The first Indian 748, BH572 flew on 1 November 1961. The first four aircraft which were Series 1s were assembled from parts made in Britain but as production developed in India, a greater and greater proportion of the aircraft (Series 2s) was made there. The final 20 aircraft benefitted from the large freight

door. Both the Indian Air Force and Indian Airways Corporation were recipients of the aircraft and 89 were licence-built in India between 1961 and 1984.

The 748 in service
The 748 first airline services were with Aerolineas Argentinas in April 1962 and the airline's order was soon increased by three to twelve in all. One of the reasons that the Argentine airline had purchased the 748 was because they needed an aircraft that offered airliner comfort but operated from undeveloped, rough airstrips as there were plenty of these on their network. The 748s flown by Aerolineas Argentinas were later joined by many others in South America and on the other side of the world. The 748 sold well in Africa too, where there were eventually 21 operators.

The 748 made headway in the very competitive market conditions in Europe earning orders from BKS, Austrian Airways and Channel Airways, Autair, British Airways and the UK's Dan-Air which had a large fleet. Canada proved a market too and 748s are still currently in use in there with Air North, Wasaya, Air Creebec and Air Inuit. The last UK airline to fly the 748

was Emerald but in 2006 it ceased trading. Bismillah in Bangladesh, still flies three 748s.

Military and executive roles
In the early 1960s Hawker Siddeley won the contract to replace the RAF's remaining Vickers Valettas, Beverleys and Hastings fleets. This led to a very substantial redesign of the 748 with a widened wing, new raised rear fuselage and tail to permit rear loading and air-dropping, strengthened freight floor and increased gross weight. It also had increased power from its Dart RDa12s, and a unique 'kneeling' undercarriage to facilitate the loading and unloading of freight.

Named the Andover, 31 were delivered to Transport Command at Abingdon commencing in July 1966. However within less than ten years the type fell victim to defence cuts. Ten were sold to the RNZAF as a Bristol 170 replacement but they were withdrawn from use in 1984. A number were prematurely scrapped while nine were converted at Woodford to become Andover E3s for radio and airport navigation aid calibration. Others were

XS605 was delivered as an Andover C1 in September 1966. It was converted to an E3 for radio and airport navigation aid calibration in 1984. *(Avro Heritage)*

employed in communications flying, at Boscombe Down and with the ETPS.

A military freighter version of the standard HS748 entered production in the 1970s with a large side-opening freight door and optional strengthened floor which could be opened in flight for paratroop or supply dropping and had accommodation for up to 58 troops. The aircraft already had rapidly interchangeable passenger, passenger/cargo and all-cargo role capabilities, but the large cargo door allowed operators to load bulkier cargo items and light vehicles. Many other military roles were undertaken by the HS748 including; aeromedical evacuation, navigation trainer and communications flying. Military 748 Operators were: Argentina, Australia, Brunei, Belgium, Brazil, Colombia, Ecuador, India, Nepal, South Korea, Thailand and Zambia.

The 748 also proved popular as a VIP and executive transport and was used as a personal aircraft by the Heads of State of

⌃ D-AFSJ flying over Woodford. It was delivered to the German Department of Flight Safety in April 1976. *(Avro Heritage)*

Argentina, Brazil, Chile, India, Thailand, Venezuela, Zambia, and the United Kingdom. It was also used as a VIP/communications aircraft by the air forces of Brazil, Australia, India and the United Kingdom.

The HS748 becomes the BAe748

Just as the Avro 748 had become the Hawker Siddeley 748 following Hawker Siddeley's rationalisation, with the formation British Aerospace in 1977 it was rebranded as the BAe 748. By then more than 250 748s were in service and flying hours were well past the two-million-hour mark. Production was then around 18 aircraft a year, mainly for military customers and for government use. Aircraft had been sold to some 60 military and civil operators, providing a firm base for re-orders. Conversion from passenger to an all-freight layout could be achieved in 15 minutes. Operating at its maximum take-off weight of 45,087lb, the 748 could carry its maximum payload of just over 11,000lb for 540nm with reserves.

In a competitive market place development had to continue and the basis for the BAe 748 2B was the uprated Dart 536 with 2,280shp fitted with 12ft propellers. Wingspan was extended to 102ft 5in and avionics and sound proofing were upgraded. G-BGJV, the

The sole Coastguarder G-BCDZ, a sensible development of the 748 which surprisingly failed to make any sales. It flew in February 1977 and was eventually converted back to a standard 748 configuration in 1980. *(Avro Heritage)*

The first BAe 748 Series 2B G-BGJV flying over Manchester. While in service with the Sri Lankan Air Force it was shot down by a SAM missile fired by Tamil separatists. (Avro Heritage)

prototype 2B (which was also fitted with a Large Freight Door) first flew on 22 June 1979. Even this development was not this sturdy airliner's last, for in 1983 BAe announced the Super 748 with yet more powerful Darts together with hush kits, greater fuel efficiency, an interior redesign

▼ The prototype ATP G-MATP and first production aircraft G-BMYM which flew in June 1986 and February 1987 respectively. (Avro Heritage)

and a more advanced flight deck. The first Super 748 G-BLGJ flew on 30 June 1984 and was displayed at Farnborough. By this time the number of deliveries had slowed to a trickle and the final 748 delivery was to Makung Airlines of Taiwan on 24 January 1989. A total of 381 748s built

and all bar the first prototype were delivered to customers.

BAe ATP – the 748 replacement

In 1980 BAe Manchester (Woodford and Chadderton) project development team seriously began planning for a 748 replacement. The 748 was one of a trio of types in 40+ seat market, the others being the De Havilland Canada Dash 7 and the Fokker F-27. For a long time 748 operators had been asking for a replacement and where a revamped 748 might have been the obvious choice by then there were several competitors in the offing; the De Havilland Canada Dash 8 and the Franco-Italian ATR42. The brand-new ATR42 was rightly focused on a large market segment of perhaps 800 aircraft in the 40-50 seat market and offered a step change in technology, primarily in terms of structural weight through its use of composites and contemporary aerodynamics, to lower operating costs.

The attitude of the BAe Board

The former Chief Test Pilot at Woodford, Robby Robinson wrote that ...."*many members of the (BAe) Board were keen to get rid of the civil side of BAe, to concentrate on the military side*".... The Board's brief to the 748 replacement team was ... "*for a minimum change from the 748 but to increase the seating capacity from 48 to 70*".

▲ BAe ATP logo.

But the Manchester team remained confident of a market for this size of aircraft and believed that the ATP (Advanced Turboprop) could achieve at least 25% of that.

Matters were then delayed for two years as the ATP's go ahead became inextricably linked to Government launch aid for the Airbus A320. The BAe Board was willing to fund the ATP if the Government provided the A320 funding. Fortunately Mrs Thatcher's Government provided £250m support for the A320 so 1 March 1984 British Aerospace gave the ATP the go ahead using internal funding. First flight was scheduled for August 1986, with deliveries beginning in 1987 but by now even more competition was on the horizon, for the Fokker 50 was due to fly in 1985.

The design

The project team options were clearly confined by the Board's decision. Thus the Advanced Turboprop or ATP had a light alloy structure based on the 748 putting it at a weight disadvantage with the ATR's composite structure. The ATP could

▲ Four of Air Europe's ATPs. The airline briefly operated a total of 17 ATPs from 1998 until 2001 when it went out of business. *(Avro Heritage)*

▼ **N851AW was the first ATP delivered to Air Wisconsin in 1990. After ten years' service, it was sold to Westair Sweden and was converted to become an ATP Freighter.** *(Avro Heritage)*

accommodate 72 rather than its predecessor's 44-48 passengers and this was achieved by lengthening the 748's fuselage by 16ft 6in both fore and aft of the wing. The wing of similar dimensions to the 748 used a strengthened version of the wider centre-section of the RAF's Andover to move the engines outboard and reduce cabin noise from the ATP's larger propellers. Whereas the 748s flying controls were retained, unlike the 748 the ATP had smaller windows though twice as many per passenger.

The reasoning behind the decision to stretch the aircraft was that BAe could not afford to build a developed 44-48 seat aircraft for a cost per seat mile that was economical. A bigger aircraft would not cost much more to build, but by stretching it could charge more and bring cost per seat down. It can be argued that the right thing to do would be to drive down costs to produce what the market wanted.

As Rolls-Royce was no longer developing turboprops, BAe chose the ▶

Pratt & Whitney Canada PW124 with 2,570 shp driving six-bladed 13ft 9in BAe / Hamilton Standard propellers, a combination which proved remarkably quiet and fuel efficient. In addition to the lengthened fuselage and for sake of appearance, rather than aerodynamics, the original 748 nose was sharpened and the vertical tail was swept back. The new aircraft had four doors with airstairs fitted to the front passenger door.

While the structure was based on the 748 with modifications, there was a wholly new electrical system, new environmental control system, revised hydraulics system and a new landing gear. The initial intention was for the UK Civil Aviation Authority to certify the ATP as a modified 748 but the inclusion of all these new systems and equipment such as EFIS and FADEC (Fully Automated Digital Engine Control) meant that the aircraft's systems were 85% new and so it had to be certified as a new type, which delayed the certification schedule.

BAe stated that development costs totalled £120m, modest compared with the other new turboprops. The ATP is 27% 748. The company claimed that had it gone for a completely new aircraft it would have cost around £350 million and produced only a 4% improvement in performance over that of the ATP.

Sales

Prior to its first flight In early 1986 the ATP's sales were poor. The ATP's rivals had been way ahead at the same point. The Fokker 50 had had 38 orders and 12 options at its first flight, while the ATR42 had 37 orders and 22 options two months before it flew. British Midland Airways had three firm orders for the ATP with two options, the first for delivery in August 1987, and Antigua-based LIAT had two on order with two options for delivery from 1988. By this time the Franco-Italian ATR42 was selling well and in 1986 the 70-seater ATR72 was announced setting this by now established new design

△ The ATP was rebranded as the Jetstream 61 and production moved to Prestwick. The first J61 completed at Prestwick was G-JLXI. (i.e. J for Jetstream and 61 in Roman numerals.) It made its maiden flight in May 1994 but with the closure of the ATP/J61 programme was scrapped three years later. *(Avro Heritage)*

▽ A close-up of the Large Freight Door fitted to the ATPF. This installation has made the ATPF into an effective freighter and eleven remain in service. *(BAE SYSTEMS)*

head-to-head against a revamped design.

First flight

The first ATP (G-MATP) painted in BAe colours made its maiden flight at 10:00 on 6 August 1986 – a date set two years earlier by Charles Masefield, former Test pilot and the Managing Director of Woodford. Masefield had rightly imposed this date when he felt that the project was beginning to run late. The weather was very bad so the prototype started its short take-off run in spray from the rain-soaked Woodford runway. The two-and-a-half-hour flight was concluded by a smooth landing in the wet, with a 24kt crosswind (the design figure was 30kt in the dry). Chief test pilot 'Robbie' Robinson reported a trouble-free flight. G-MATP appeared at the Farnborough Air Show and impressed onlookers with its low noise level, due primarily to its six-blade, slow-speed propellers.

With the hardware in the air BAe was confident that the aircraft would begin to make an impact on the civil market, and the company continued to study military

applications in maritime patrol and AEW. There was also a continuing dialogue with the USSR on sales of the ATP for intercity use, which regrettably came to naught.

The second aircraft G-BMYM painted in British Midland's livery did not fly until six months after the prototype, in February 1987. The third ATP, G-BMYK also in British Midland livery, flew in June that year. G-MATP was tasked with clearing handling and cold trials in Finland and Iceland, aircraft number two, systems and hot and high trials in Spain and Arizona while the third ATP (a furnished aircraft) backed up these programmes and conducted tests on the environmental control system, cabin noise, evacuation procedures and 200hr of route proving. Certification of the ATP was granted in March 1988 and included 1,290hr of flying with three aircraft in Finland, Iceland, Spain, and the USA as well as in the UK.

Sales and service

The ATP started working for its living on 9 May 1988. The first operator of the type, British Midland (BMA), flew its maiden commercial sortie out of Birmingham for Brussels at the beginning of a planned eight-sector day, which included schedules to the Channel Islands and another rotation to Brussels. Unfortunately, in the same month, Wings West an American Eagle feeder carrier cancelled its order for ten. However American FAA certification followed in late 1988 and the following year in what seemed a breakthrough, Air Wisconsin ordered 14 with deliveries from 1989 to 1991, but ceased operations with the type in 2000.

In March 1988 just prior to the ATP's entry into service British Airways ordered eight and eventually operated a fleet of 14 on regional services from January 1989 until early 1999. Another UK carrier, Manx Airlines, a subsidiary of BMA took over BMA's ATPs and became a major operator of the ATP with a fleet eventually totalling 17 which served from 1989 to 1995. Other operators included the Azorean operator

▲ ATP Freighter G-BTPH in service with West Atlantic Cargo Airlines. *(BAE SYSTEMS)*

SATA, Air Europa, Biman Bangladesh Airlines, British World Airlines, Loganair, and Merpati of Indonesia. The aircraft initially had problems with its engine/gearbox, de-icing and undercarriage but these were all eventually cured.

The ATP becomes the Jetstream 61

In January 1993 the management of British Aerospace decided to transfer all aspects of the ATP to Jetstream Aircraft Ltd, BAe's turboprop subsidiary based at Prestwick (the former Scottish Aviation factory). This placed production of all British Aerospace's turboprop aircraft at one centre. Production of the ATP was now alongside that of the Jetstream 31 and 41. To reinforce the branding in April 1993 BAe announced that the ATP was

renamed the Jetstream 61.

Plans were announced at the 1993 Paris Air Show to expand the range of Jetstream Aircraft's offerings with a Jetstream 51 and Jetstream 71. These would have passenger capacity less than and greater than the Jetstream 61 respectively. BAe made it clear that these projects could only go ahead on a collaborative basis. Neither type was developed.

The first Jetstream 61 to be assembled at Prestwick was the 64th aircraft, registered G-JLXI. It made its maiden flight on 10 May 1994 and appeared at the 1994 Farnborough Air Show in a dynamic livery. Modifications incorporated on the Jetstream 61 were more powerful Pratt & Whitney 127Ds of 2,750shp, an improved interior with larger luggage lockers and

an increase in operating weights.

The prototype ATP G-MATP had already flown on 21 June 1993 with the higher-powered Pratt & Whitney PW127D engines. Following ATP's rebranding as the Jetstream 61 it was re-registered on 26 August 1994 as G-PLXI and flew in J61 livery.

The end of production

In January 1995 BAe decided to combine with Aerospatiale (now EADS) of France and Alenia (now Leonardo) of Italy to form the European regional aircraft consortium, Aero International (Regional) to jointly market their regional aircraft. This put the Jetstream 61 in direct competition with the very successful Aerospatiale/Alenia ATR42/72.

The Jetstream 61 was certified in mid-June 1995 and the second J61 (G11-065) flew the following month. BAe was still intending to sell six J61s before closing the production line but none of the Prestwick-built aircraft was sold. So the two completed J61s and 13 more in various states of completion on the Prestwick and Chadderton production lines were scrapped. Altogether only 65 ATPs/J61s were built and the last two never even went into service.

The ATP Freighter

In 2000 BAE Systems Asset Management, which then owned 40 ATPs, launched the ➤

Data	748 Series 2B	ATP
Length	67 ft	85 ft 4 in
Wingspan	98 ft 6in	100 ft 6 in
Height	24 ft 10 in	23ft 5in
MTOW	46,500 lb	50,550 lb
Cruising speed	281 mph	306 mph
Range	904 mls	1,134 mls
Passengers	44-62	72
Powerplant	2 x 2,280hp Rolls-Royce Dart R.Da.7 Mk 536-2	2 x 2,570hp Pratt & Whitney Canada PW124

ATPF Freighter project. This offered both bulk 'E' class and Large Freight Door versions (LFD). The ATPF is a true 8-tonne plus freighter, capable of carrying eight LD3 containers or six LD4s when fitted with the Large Freight Door, or bulk loading of up to eight tonnes when configured with an E-Class compartment.

The first ATPF fitted with the LFD, SE-LGZ flew from West Atlantic Airlines' base at Linkoping in Sweden on 10 July 2002. In total 23 ATPs were fitted with LFDs while 20 ATPs were converted to the bulk role with E-Class interiors. Eleven ATPFs are still operated throughout Europe and to North Africa by West Atlantic Airlines, and two more are operating in Indonesia with Deraya Air Services. Only five pure passenger versions remain in operation with NextJet of Sweden.

Conclusion

The steady development and refinement of the 748, maintained demand for the aircraft and amply repaid Hawker Siddeley for risking its capital. If BAe had launched a 748 upgrade with the same seating capacity earlier, it could have done as well as the Fokker 50, especially if it had come to market ahead of the ATR. But by the time that the ATP finally arrived in 1988, the ATR42 had gathered many orders, with the Fokker 50 coming a creditable second. Ironically the ATP then found itself head-to-head with the larger ATR72, the latter now based on the proven and highly successful ATR42 and with a growing customer base compared to the rapidly declining 748 community, many of whom of course had already switched to the smaller ATR.

The ATP failed to match the performance and economics of the ATR. The ATP cruised slower than the ATR owing to using the 748 wing, by then approximately thirty years old. The ATP could only compete by adding more power, which was offered but came at a cost of increased fuel burn and engine maintenance costs. However the ATP has performed well as a freighter and accessed a market that at the time the ATR72 could not match, given its much higher cost. The structure of the ATP is very robust and the door design very simple compared to the more complex powered door of the ATR freighter. ∎

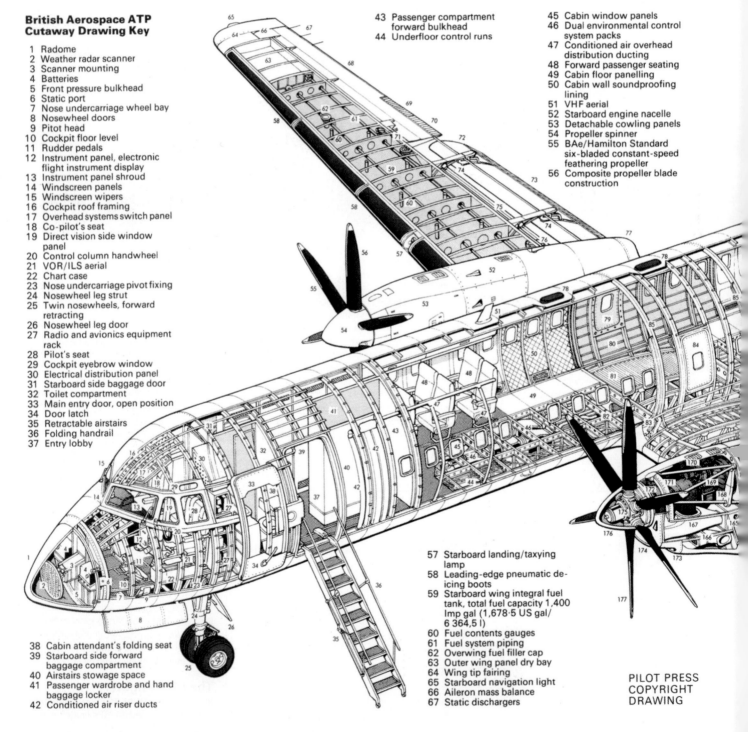

British Aerospace ATP Cutaway Drawing Key

1 Radome
2 Weather radar scanner
3 Scanner mounting
4 Batteries
5 Front pressure bulkhead
6 Static port
7 Nose undercarriage wheel bay
8 Nosewheel doors
9 Pitot head
10 Cockpit floor level
11 Rudder pedals
12 Instrument panel, electronic flight instrument display
13 Instrument panel shroud
14 Windscreen panels
15 Windscreen wipers
16 Cockpit roof framing
17 Overhead systems switch panel
18 Co-pilot's seat
19 Direct vision side window panel
20 Control column handwheel
21 VOR/ILS aerial
22 Chart case
23 Nose undercarriage pivot fixing
24 Nosewheel leg strut
25 Twin nosewheels, forward retracting
26 Nosewheel leg door
27 Radio and avionics equipment rack
28 Pilot's seat
29 Cockpit eyebrow window
30 Electrical distribution panel
31 Starboard side baggage door
32 Toilet compartment
33 Main entry door, open position
34 Door latch
35 Retractable airstairs
36 Folding handrail
37 Entry lobby

38 Cabin attendant's folding seat
39 Starboard side forward baggage compartment
40 Airstairs stowage space
41 Passenger wardrobe and hand baggage locker
42 Conditioned air riser ducts

43 Passenger compartment forward bulkhead
44 Underfloor control runs

45 Cabin window panels
46 Dual environmental control system packs
47 Conditioned air overhead distribution ducting
48 Forward passenger seating
49 Cabin floor panelling
50 Cabin wall soundproofing lining
51 VHF aerial
52 Starboard engine nacelle
53 Detachable cowling panels
54 Propeller spinner
55 BAe/Hamilton Standard six-bladed constant-speed feathering propeller
56 Composite propeller blade construction

57 Starboard landing/taxying lamp
58 Leading-edge pneumatic de-icing boots
59 Starboard wing integral fuel tank, total fuel capacity 1,400 Imp gal (1,678·5 US gal/ 6 364,5 l)
60 Fuel contents gauges
61 Fuel system piping
62 Overwing fuel filler cap
63 Outer wing panel dry bay
64 Wing tip fairing
65 Starboard navigation light
66 Aileron mass balance
67 Static dischargers

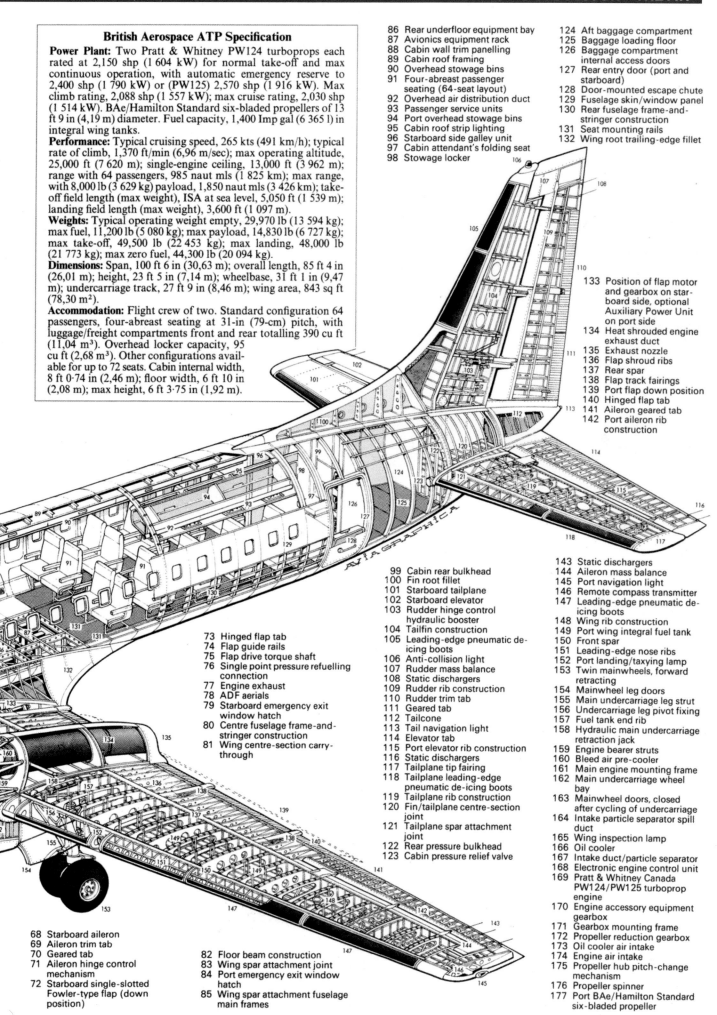

British Aerospace ATP Specification

Power Plant: Two Pratt & Whitney PW124 turboprops each rated at 2,150 shp (1 604 kW) for normal take-off and max continuous operation, with automatic emergency reserve to 2,400 shp (1 790 kW) or (PW125) 2,570 shp (1 916 kW). Max climb rating, 2,088 shp (1 557 kW); max cruise rating, 2,030 shp (1 514 kW). BAe/Hamilton Standard six-bladed propellers of 13 ft 9 in (4,19 m) diameter. Fuel capacity, 1,400 Imp gal (6 365 l) in integral wing tanks.

Performance: Typical cruising speed, 265 kts (491 km/h); typical rate of climb, 1,370 ft/min (6,96 m/sec); max operating altitude, 25,000 ft (7 620 m); single-engine ceiling, 13,000 ft (3 962 m); range with 64 passengers, 985 naut mls (1 825 km); max range, with 8,000 lb (3 629 kg) payload, 1,850 naut mls (3 426 km); take-off field length (max weight), ISA at sea level, 5,050 ft (1 539 m); landing field length (max weight), 3,600 ft (1 097 m).

Weights: Typical operating weight empty, 29,970 lb (13 594 kg); max fuel, 11,200 lb (5 080 kg); max payload, 14,830 lb (6 727 kg); max take-off, 49,500 lb (22 453 kg); max landing, 48,000 lb (21 773 kg); max zero fuel, 44,300 lb (20 094 kg).

Dimensions: Span, 100 ft 6 in (30,63 m); overall length, 85 ft 4 in (26,01 m); height, 23 ft 5 in (7,14 m); wheelbase, 31 ft 1 in (9,47 m); undercarriage track, 27 ft 9 in (8,46 m); wing area, 843 sq ft (78,30 m²).

Accommodation: Flight crew of two. Standard configuration 64 passengers, four-abreast seating at 31-in (79-cm) pitch, with luggage/freight compartments front and rear totalling 390 cu ft (11,04 m³). Overhead locker capacity, 95 cu ft (2,68 m³). Other configurations available for up to 72 seats. Cabin internal width, 8 ft 0.74 in (2,46 m); floor width, 6 ft 10 in (2,08 m); max height, 6 ft 3.75 in (1,92 m).

86 Rear underfloor equipment bay
87 Avionics equipment rack
88 Cabin wall trim panelling
89 Cabin roof framing
90 Overhead stowage bins
91 Four-abreast passenger seating (64-seat layout)
92 Overhead air distribution duct
93 Passenger service units
94 Port overhead stowage bins
95 Cabin roof strip lighting
96 Starboard side galley unit
97 Cabin attendant's folding seat
98 Stowage locker

124 Aft baggage compartment
125 Baggage loading floor
126 Baggage compartment internal access doors
127 Rear entry door (port and starboard)
128 Door-mounted escape chute
129 Fuselage skin/window panel
130 Rear fuselage frame-and-stringer construction
131 Seat mounting rails
132 Wing root trailing-edge fillet

133 Position of flap motor and gearbox on starboard side, optional Auxiliary Power Unit on port side
134 Heat shrouded engine exhaust duct
135 Exhaust nozzle
136 Flap shroud ribs
137 Rear spar
138 Flap track fairings
139 Port flap down position
140 Hinged flap tab
141 Aileron geared tab
142 Port aileron rib construction

99 Cabin rear bulkhead
100 Fin root fillet
101 Starboard tailplane
102 Starboard elevator
103 Rudder hinge control hydraulic booster
104 Tailfin construction
105 Leading-edge pneumatic de-icing boots
106 Anti-collision light
107 Rudder mass balance
108 Static dischargers
109 Rudder rib construction
110 Rudder trim tab
111 Geared tab
112 Tailcone
113 Tail navigation light
114 Elevator tab
115 Port elevator rib construction
116 Static dischargers
117 Tailplane tip fairing
118 Tailplane leading-edge pneumatic de-icing boots
119 Tailplane rib construction
120 Fin/tailplane centre-section joint
121 Tailplane spar attachment joint
122 Rear pressure bulkhead
123 Cabin pressure relief valve

143 Static dischargers
144 Aileron mass balance
145 Port navigation light
146 Remote compass transmitter
147 Leading-edge pneumatic de-icing boots
148 Wing rib construction
149 Port wing integral fuel tank
150 Front spar
151 Leading-edge nose ribs
152 Port landing/taxiing lamp
153 Twin mainwheels, forward retracting
154 Mainwheel leg doors
155 Main undercarriage leg strut
156 Undercarriage leg pivot fixing
157 Fuel tank end rib
158 Hydraulic main undercarriage retraction jack
159 Engine bearer struts
160 Bleed air pre-cooler
161 Main engine mounting frame
162 Main undercarriage wheel bay
163 Mainwheel doors, closed after cycling of undercarriage
164 Intake particle separator spill duct
165 Wing inspection lamp
166 Oil cooler
167 Intake duct/particle separator
168 Electronic engine control unit
169 Pratt & Whitney Canada PW124/PW125 turboprop engine
170 Engine accessory equipment gearbox
171 Gearbox mounting frame
172 Propeller reduction gearbox
173 Oil cooler air intake
174 Engine air intake
175 Propeller hub pitch-change mechanism
176 Propeller spinner
177 Port BAe/Hamilton Standard six-bladed propeller

73 Hinged flap tab
74 Flap guide rails
75 Flap drive torque shaft
76 Single point pressure refuelling connection
77 Engine exhaust
78 ADF aerials
79 Starboard emergency exit window hatch
80 Centre fuselage frame-and-stringer construction
81 Wing centre-section carry-through

68 Starboard aileron
69 Aileron trim tab
70 Geared tab
71 Aileron hinge control mechanism
72 Starboard single-slotted Fowler-type flap (down position)

82 Floor beam construction
83 Wing spar attachment joint
84 Port emergency exit window hatch
85 Wing spar attachment fuselage main frames

Executive best-seller – the 125

After selling more than 500 piston-engined de Havilland Doves, Hatfield began designing a jet replacement in 1961 powered by the Bristol Siddeley Viper. The first prototype, G-ARYA flew from Hatfield in August 1962 and the second 'RYB in December. The first production aircraft G-ARYC, a 125 Series 1 which flew in February 1963 was the first 125 assembled and flown from Broughton.

The 125 was a conventional design whose fuselage sat almost entirely atop a low, moderately swept 47ft wing. Fitting

▲ G-ARYA, the prototype de Havilland (later Hawker Siddeley) 125 having ground trials at Hatfield prior to its maiden flight on 13 August 1962. This aircraft was one foot shorter and its wingspan was three foot less than the production aircraft. *(BAE SYSTEMS)*

the wing in this manner provided a flat cabin floor and aisle with headroom of 69 inches able to accommodate six to ten passengers. Entrance was via a single door which opened up and over on the inside. The compact flightdeck had seating and controls for two pilots but could be flown by one. To maintain simplicity all the flying controls were manually operated and the wing had air brakes and double-slotted flaps.

In demand around the world
Orders mounted up speedily and by mid-1963 the 125 already had 36 firm

orders from the batch of sixty which had been laid down. Of these, the RAF was to receive 20 for navigational training. More orders soon followed. G-ASSI embarked on a 105-day tour of North America which was so successful that 22 orders were received. Those 125s destined for North America were completed at Broughton unpainted, unfurnished, with bare walls and fitted with rudimentary avionics for delivery to a Distributor's Completion Centre on the other side of the Atlantic.

Military 125s
The RAF's 20 125s, named Dominie T1 by the RAF, were navigation trainers and the full fleet were in service by mid-1966. They were specially versioned for this role with a comprehensive navigation panel with appropriate avionics at the rear fuselage bulkhead. Eleven aircraft from the original order of 20 were put through a Mid-Life-Update programme beginning in 1992 to upgrade and modernise the jets and to make them more appropriate for training crews on modern fast jet fleets. They were withdrawn from use in January 2011.

Over 20 Governments operated 125s in VIP or support roles including No 32 Squadron based at RAF Northolt, which eventually had twelve aircraft. In the late 1990s 125s were also purchased as flight inspection aircraft by seven countries including the USA and Japan.

RAF Dominie XS728 leaving Cambridge after a major systems update by Marshall's in August 1995. *(BAE SYSTEMS)*

HB-VDL, a 125-600 registered in Lichtenstein and owned by German dress manufacturer Müller-Wipperfürth from 1973 until 1976. *(BAE SYSTEMS)*

Developing the 125

The strong sales outlook for the 125 encouraged Hawker Siddeley to develop it further and produce a 125 Series 3 which had detail improvements over the Series 1 (the RAF Dominie was the Series 2), better air-conditioning, APU and furnishing. Some Series 3 had an external ventral fuel tank which fitted neatly under the rear fuselage to extend the aircraft's range. Following on from the Series 3 came the Series 400 (henceforward all new Series were in 100s) which had the entrance door re-engineered, freeing up space within the cabin.

Sales grow

The 125 was one of only two European-built bizjets to have been widely adopted by North American operators, the other being the Dassault Falcon. In 1968 50 125s were sold and 44 the following year. By then sales had reached 228 and of these sales, 132 had been to US and Canadian customers, representing 57% of the total. The remaining 54 were sold to other overseas countries; 22 to UK operators; and 20 to the RAF as Dominies. Amongst those UK sales were two delivered to BAC for communications flying on their collaborative programmes, one aircraft based at Filton flying daily to Toulouse for Concorde liaison and the other shuttling between Warton and Munich for Tornado co-operation.

More power leads to the 125-600

The 125-600 which succeeded the 125-400 had more powerful and economical Viper 601s, plus a 2ft fuselage extension increasing maximum passenger capacity to 14. It had better airfield performance, could cruise at slightly higher speeds and with its fuel capacity

▲ To celebrate the sale of the 400th 125 there was a line-up of twelve 125s and a further one in the background at BAe Broughton on 20 April 1978. The 125s were; G-BFAN, G-AVOI, G-5-13, G-BBEP, XS730, G-BSAA, XW791, unknown, XW930, G-BARB, G-BEFZ, G-AWWL and G-BJCB. The Dan-Air HS748 is G-ATMI. *(BAE SYSTEMS)*

increased by the addition of a fin tank had a range of up to 1,875 mls. However, owing to the introduction of noise regulations in the USA and Europe a 'hush kit' was fitted to the Viper 601s on some aircraft but did not prove to be very effective. So because of the noisiness of the Rolls-Royce Viper 601s and the increase in world oil prices, the 600 series only made 71 sales.

The Turbofan 125-700

Despite concerns about the costs and the threat of nationalisation of the aircraft industry by the Labour Government, Hawker Siddeley financed the re-engining of the 125. As there was no Rolls-Royce

engine available the American-built Garrett TFE731 was selected. This engine offered 3,700lbs thrust; the noise footprint was reduced by 80% and the greatly improved fuel consumption almost doubled the 125's range.

The second prototype 125-600 G-AZHS was re-engined as the Series 700 prototype and suitably re-registered as G-BFAN flew in July 1976. The first production aircraft was G-BEFZ which made its maiden flight in November 1976 and was based at Hatfield for test flying and then flew on a worldwide Sales Tour. Though aircraft were still designated as 125-700A for North America and 700B for the remainder of

➤

the world, gradually the specification of the latter had been brought up to the higher specification of the North American model and so the differences between them diminished.

BAe and the best-selling 125

Amongst the early decisions facing British Aerospace was further development of the 125 to maintain their market share. Such was demand for

▼ The first of six 125-800s ordered as flight inspection C-29As for the USAF on the production line at BAe Broughton in 1989. The Japanese Self-Defence Force ordered similar aircraft.
(BAE SYSTEMS)

the 125-700 that potential customers had to join a nine-month waiting list. In 1979 sales exceeded targets and 55 were sold in October 1980 and BAe celebrated the sale of the 500th 125 which also had the distinction of being the 300th sold in the USA.

As sales were booming and the 125 was third in the small executive jet market behind the American Learjet and Cessna Citation in 1980, the BAe Board

gave the go ahead for the 125-800. The 800 was a major redesign of the whole aircraft which made it look far more attractive. It had a redesigned tail, new outboard wings giving an increase in wing span of 4½ft and deeper fuselage. Profile changes to the nose, windscreen and canopy improved pilot visibility and an EFIS flightdeck was fitted. Overall fuel capacity was greater and with its 3,000ml range the 125-800 could easily fly coast-to-coast across the USA. To power the 800, the more powerful TFE-731-5R offered 4,300lbs was chosen.

On 1 June 1983 for its public debut the 125-800 had a ceremonial roll out and demonstration flight from Broughton painted as N800BA. Its actual maiden flight had been made the week before, unpainted, registered as G-5-11. Registered as G-BKTF it carried out the bulk of the 125-800's nine-month test programme from Hatfield. The second prototype G-DCCC (DCCC = 800 in Roman numerals) joined the first in June 1983, was used as a BAe demonstrator and later sold. Certification of the new 125 was granted in the spring of 1984.

Scheduled production was 28 aircraft per annum with approximately 60% going to the United States, 20% in the UK and the remainder around the world. Yet not all sales were as executive jets. In 1988 the USAF chose the 125-800 as C-29A for the Combat Flight Inspection and Navigation role and the Japanese Air Self-Defence Force followed suit. This order paved the way for an order for 27 radically-altered U-125A which fulfilled a Japanese Search and Rescue role. These aircraft were the most heavily modified versions of the 125, with a large observer's window ahead of the wing on both sides of the fuselage and the ability to drop life raft. Flying below 1,500ft at 150 knots a cover over the left wheel is unscrewed, a raft placed in it, the undercarriage extended and the life raft drops, inflating on contact with the sea.

The 125-1000

The last stretch to the 125 was the 125-1000, an 800 with a 33inch stretch to the fuselage married to a new engine, the Pratt & Whitney PW305 with 5,225lbs thrust. The improved dimensions were reflected in cabin improvements. The BAe 125-1000 prototype, G-AEXLR made its first flight on 16 June 1990 and was soon joined by two more test aircraft; G-OPFC and the first production aircraft G-ELRA. Unable to fully achieve its range estimates the 125-1000 failed to emulate the 125-800 and only 52 BAe 125-1000s were built.

Change of ownership – from BAe to Raytheon

Throughout the early 1990s British Aerospace had major financial problems, and began investigating sales of some of its core businesses. So the 125 programme became a stand-alone company known as BAe Corporate Jets, then earning approximately £300m per year and employing 950 in the UK.

It was offered for sale and was bought by in 1993 Raytheon, an American firm for £250m.

Raytheon rebranded the aircraft as the Hawker and introduced the Hawker 800XP (Extended Performance) an 800 with essentially the wing of the 1000, 4,650lb-thrust Garrett TFE731-5BR turbofans with thrust reversers, new systems, interior and more fuel capacity. In 2006 came two new variants the Hawker 750 and the 900XP. The 750 had more storage but less range than the 800XP. The Hawker 900XP offered greater range than the 850XP with its TFE731-50R 4,660lbs thrust engines and could fly non-stop from London City airport to Goose Bay in Canada with six passengers. The fuselage, wings and

vertical tail were still assembled and partially equipped at Airbus Broughton but final assembly was gradually transferred to Wichita, Kansas. Production of the Hawker (or 125) ended in 2012 after a business restructuring at Hawker Beechcraft.

Altogether 944 125s were produced in the UK, and when production terminated after 50 years and with a grand total of 1,731 built, the 125 was clearly the most prolific of all UK jet civil aircraft. ∎

Data	BAe 125-800
Length	51 ft 2 in
Wingspan	51 ft 5 in
Height	17 ft 7 in
MTOW	27,400 lbs
Cruising speed	510 mph
Range	2,450 mls
Passengers	Max. 14
Engine	Garrett TFE731 4,300lbs thrust

The fourth BAe 125-1000 G-LRBJ which flew in 1991. The 125-1000, was 33 inches longer than the 125-800 with a new engine, the Pratt & Whitney PW305 with 5,225lbs thrust. *(BAE SYSTEMS)*

Jetstream reborn

∧ Roll out of the first Jetstream prototype G-ATXH at Handley Page's factory at Radlett in August 1967. *(Author's collection)*

Scottish Aviation was producing Bulldog primary trainers (which it had taken on after Beagle's bankruptcy), C-130 fuselage sections, overhauling piston engines for Rolls-Royce and was finishing off a contract to build Jetstreams for the RAF. The Jetstream was a Handley Page design and this work had come to Prestwick owing to its original involvement with it, manufacturing the wings.

Once it became part of British Aerospace in April 1977 Prestwick did benefit from comparatively small packages of work but what Scottish Aviation most wanted to secure was to launch and develop a new version of the Jetstream.

The Handley Page Jetstream

The Handley Page Aircraft Company, originally formed in 1909, was a manufacturer of large military and civil aircraft. By the late 1950s Government policy was to force aircraft firms to merge into larger units. Having failed to join either Hawker Siddeley or BAC, the future was poor for Handley Page as the firm had no prospect of winning Government contracts.

Thanks to legacy programmes such as the superb Victor 'V' bomber the company had time to examine projects that would not stretch its financial resources. Handley Page went ahead and designed a pressurised, low wing civil aircraft powered by twin turboprops capable of transporting 18 passengers in a three-abreast layout. This was launched in January 1966 as the HP137 Jetstream, tailored to fill a gap in the feeder-liner market aimed primarily at the United States.

As there was no suitable British engine in the required power range, the French Turboméca Astazou 14 of 840hp was chosen for the Jetstream production aircraft. The prototype, G-ATXH, flew from Handley Page's Hertfordshire factory at Radlett for the first time in August 1967. Besides engine problems, the aircraft was overweight, and drag was higher than calculated. These problems all led to a delay in certification and an increase in costs far greater than the original estimate

Two Jetstreams built or substantially built at Radlett. Scottish Aviation assembled part Handley Page-built RAF Jetstream T1 XX488 and Handley Page-built Royal Navy Jetstream T2 ZA110. *(BAE SYSTEMS)*

The prototype Jetstream 31 G-TALL made its maiden flight on 18 March 1982 at Prestwick. *(BAE SYSTEMS)*

▲ Jetstream Prestwick logo

which Handley Page could ill afford.

While endeavouring to sort out the aircraft's technical problems Handley Page was also engaged in work for a large USAF order and had received a contract to produce eleven Jetstream 3Ms powered by the American Garrett AirResearch TPE-331. To hasten development of the USAF version the two Jetstreams flew with the Garrett engines. The parallel effort poured into fulfilling the USAF order for this substantially modified aircraft created a further drain on over-stretched resources.

Handley Page falls into receivership

In February 1970 Handley Page Aircraft went out of business. Over 50 Jetstreams had already been delivered to North America and several companies had begun to market the aircraft. Some

aircraft were re-engined with Pratt & Whitney PT6As and others with Garrett TPE-331s. An assortment of these continued flying with ten airlines and helped the eventual BAe Jetstream's sales success in North America.

Jetstream Aircraft and Scottish Aviation

Fortunately, the Jetstream was kept alive by interested parties and former Handley Page staff who formed a company called Jetstream Aircraft. Three completed Jetstreams, 21 engineless airframes and a large quantity of spares and design authority were purchased from Handley Page's receivers. This nascent firm used Jetstream 200 G-AXFV to achieve

certification for this development and kept the project alive, based at Sywell airport, Northamptonshire.

Jetstream Aircraft proposed a version of the Jetstream 200 for the RAF as a training aircraft. RAF evaluation trials followed from 9 August – 2 September 1971 at the A&AEE Boscombe Down with the Jetstream in competition against the Turbo Commander. Jetstream Aircraft and Scottish Aviation at Prestwick (to which HP had originally sub-contracted the building of the wings) agreed to act together as it was clear that the former had insufficient resources to take on a production contract. Against stiff American competition in February 1972 the Government awarded a contract for ➤

➤ Jetstream 31 G-OBEA entered service with Birmingham Executive Airways in May 1983 and flew with the airline until October 1992. *(BAE SYSTEMS)*

26 Jetstreams to be built by Scottish Aviation and the company bought out Jetstream Aircraft's interest in the aircraft. Scottish Aviation furnished the contract using 19 aircraft stored at Sywell, with two repatriated from the USA and five newly-built aircraft to complete the order.

The first of these, XX483 a flew on 13 April 1973 and the last was delivered in December 1976. Scottish Aviation was eager to build on its Jetstream experience and sought means to re-open production after completion of the delivery of the Jetstream T1s to the RAF. Fortunately, the company was assisted in its endeavours when it received a contract to modify 12 of the RAF's Jetstream T1s into T2

▲ PanAm's J31 N3142 with the dorsal luggage pannier fitted to many aircraft. *(BAE SYSTEMS)*

▼ Jetstream 41 – changes from Jetstream 31. *(BAE SYSTEMS)*

navigation trainers for the Royal Navy, assuring work until June 1979. (The Navy's aircraft served for 32 years and six aircraft performed a final flypast at RNAS Culdrose on 11 March 2011.)

British Aerospace and the Jetstream 31

On 5 December 1978, the newly-formed and state-owned British Aerospace decided to re-launch a new version - the Jetstream 31. However as the BAe Board was very doubtful about the likely success of the Jetstream it only agreed to the development and testing of a single aircraft and the ordering in of long-lead items for possible production.

The new BAe Jetstream 31 was based on the HP Jetstream 200 but the disappointing Astazou engines were replaced by the Garrett TPE331 - as originally flown in the USAF version by Handley Page, albeit in an amended configuration. BAe's decision was based on market research, primarily in the USA, which indicated with just a 5% share of the market there would be steady stream of orders. During the decade from the launch of the HP Jetstream there had been a burgeoning demand for 15-20 seater aircraft. It was evident that the original HP specification with its pressurised cabin and six-foot cabin height offering airline seating for 19 (or an

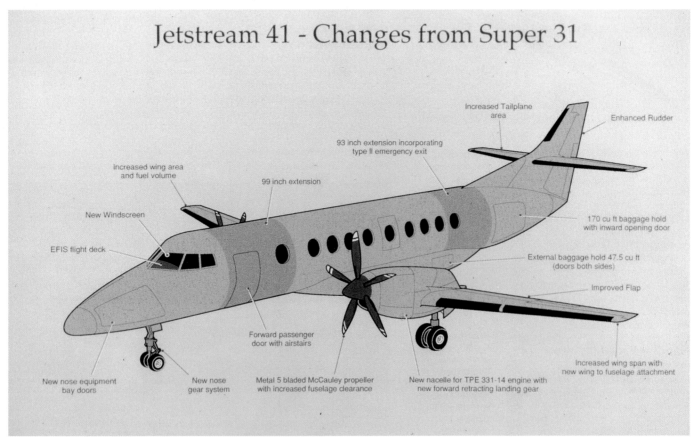

Jetstream 41 - Changes from Super 31

Increased Tailplane area

Enhanced Rudder

93 inch extension incorporating type II emergency exit

Increased wing area and fuel volume

99 inch extension

New Windscreen

170 cu ft baggage hold with inward opening door

EFIS flight deck

External baggage hold 47.5 cu ft (doors both sides)

Improved Flap

Forward passenger door with airstairs

Increased wing span with new wing to fuselage attachment

New nose equipment bay doors

New nose gear system

Metal 5 bladed McCauley propeller with increased fuselage clearance

New nacelle for TPE 331-14 engine with new forward retracting landing gear

8-12 passenger corporate layout) appealed to the market.

Prototype Jetstream 31

The 27th production HP Jetstream 1 was purchased by BAe and ferried from Natchez, USA on 26 December 1978 to Prestwick for conversion to become the prototype Jetstream 31. The main aspect of the conversion was the replacement of the Astazou engines with 940hp Garrett TPE331. In addition there were a further 400 modifications including a new electrical system and completely redesigned flight deck. It first flew as a Jetstream 31 registered as G-JSSD at Prestwick on 28 March 1980 and immediately embarked on the flight test programme.

Production batch

In January 1981, the BAe Board finally approved the production of the first batch of twenty aircraft. The first of these, G-TALL made its maiden flight on 18 March and received UK certification on 29 June, as the greater part of the flight test programme had been completed by G-JSSD. In November 1982, it toured the USA performing 30 demonstration flights, followed in March 1983 by a two-month long tour of the Middle East, Far East and Asia.

The next Jetstream 31 flew in May

▲ The Jetstream 41 prototype quartet; G-OXL1, G-GCJL, G-PJRT and G-JMAC. The first Jetstream 41, G-GCJL flew from Prestwick on 25 September 1991. The second prototype G-PJRT took to the air in February 1992. Next came G-OXLI in March 1992 and finally G-JMAC in July 1992. *(BAE SYSTEMS)*

▼ **A publicity shot of a Jetstream 41 and a 31 together flying over the BAe Prestwick factory.** *(The registrations of both aircraft have been removed.)* *(BAE SYSTEMS)*

1982 and was ferried straight to Castle Donnington (now East Midlands Airport) where Fields Aircraft Services which had won the Jetstream completion contract installed a commuter interior. Registered as G-JBAE made demonstration tours of a Europe, Canada and the USA. In 1983 prior to delivery to Atlantis Airways it

trialled a dorsal luggage pannier later fitted to many aircraft. Orders proved slow to build up but by the end of 1983 it was clear that the Jetstream was set to succeed. The BAe Board authorised regular increases in production. The Jetstream 31 was promoted as 18/19 seat airliner, an executive shuttle with up to 12 ➤

on board or an executive aircraft with an even smaller number but in greater luxury.

In service

The first J31 delivered new to the USA was the fifth aircraft, registered N331JS. It staged on its 4,600ml flight via Reykjavik, Narssarssuag, Goose Bay, Montreal and Windsor to Little Rock, Arkansas where it was handed over to a completion contractor. Over 16 weeks it was fitted out with an executive 8/9 seat interior. In the meantime, the first customer to put the aircraft into operation was German-owned Contactair. Early UK operators included McAlpine Aviation and Birmingham Executive. In 1983 the Jetstream 31 received 44 orders establishing itself throughout Europe and in North America where it proved very successful. Some J31s appeared in the colours of BA as franchise partners, such as Danish commuter airline, Sun-Air which had nine J31s and two of the larger J41s.

At the height of its popularity it wore the liveries of Eastern, PanAm, United, American, Northwest, TWA and USAir. To maintain its market position the Jetstream Super 31 (aka Jetstream 32) was announced at the 1987 Paris Air show with up-rated 1,020hp TPE-331s engines, increased cruising speed, higher operating weights, double the range and with improved cabin comfort. It also has emergency windows each side of the fuselage. Production of the J31 and J32 took place in tandem from April to October 1988 when all aircraft were completed to J32 standard.

On 24 May 1989 WestAir placed an order for 37 J31s with options on a further 15 taking total orders to over 300. But in 1992 orders began to dry up, production slowed and stopped at Prestwick by the end of 1993. Two uncompleted aircraft remained at Prestwick, the final one of these flying in May 1997.

G-MAJP flew with Eastern Airways from 2006 until 2011 and now flies with EasyFly in Costa Rica. Both Eastern Airways and EasyFly are large operators of the J41. This photo shows how the Jetstream 41's fin was increased in size after initial flight testing. *(BAE SYSTEMS)*

▼ This J41 A6-ESK now flies with SAMA Airlines in the United Arab Emirates. *(BAE SYSTEMS)*

The lengthened Jetstream 41

Encouraged by the success of the Jetstream 31 BAe had decided to develop the design further and launched the Jetstream 41 in 1989. The fuselage was lengthened with an 8ft 3in plug forward of the wing and a 7ft 9in aft increasing its length to 63ft 2in to accommodate 29 passengers. In addition to providing the space for ten more passengers, the extension allowed the introduction of a forward cabin door incorporating air stairs. A large door at the rear gave access to an enlarged luggage hold. Unlike the J31 where the wing-fuselage junction led to the protrusion of the main spar into the cabin aisle the J41's wing was attached beneath the fuselage.

The Jetstream 41 was a major alteration of the original design with more powerful AlliedSignal TPE331 1500hp turboprops in new nacelles with five-bladed propellers. The revised nacelles were utilised in the stowage of the twin-wheel main undercarriage units which retracted into them unlike the inwards into the wing as on the J31. The J41 had EFIS glass displays, a reprofiled cockpit window layout. With all these modifications, the Jetstream 41 was certified as a new aircraft.

Development of the aircraft was a three-way risk share with BAe investing £100m and Field Aircraft and Swiss manufacturer, Pilatus contributing £30m. Field's was tasked with designing and

building the aircraft's interior, with Pilatus responsible for the manufacture of tail assembly, flaps and ailerons. Later Gulfstream Aerospace Technologies of Oklahoma was contracted to design and make the wings but as work dropped off at the Prestwich plant, these agreements were terminated and all work brought in-house.

First flight

In order to complete the flight test programme as speedily as possible the first four aircraft were allotted to the task. The first Jetstream 41, G-GCJL flew from Prestwick on 25 September 1991 and was delivered to BAe's Woodford Flight Test Centre, near Manchester in November. It was initially employed on general handling trials and later icing and cold weather systems trials. The second prototype G-PJRT took to the air in February 1992 and underwent 'hot and high' trials in Arizona. It was also exhibited at the 1992 Farnborough Air Show.

Next came G-OXLI in March 1992 which was engaged in EFIS and autopilot trials and finally G-JMAC came in July 1992. G-JMAC was exhibited at both the 1993 Paris and 1994 Farnborough Air Shows. In June 1999 after J41 production had ended it was employed on steep approach certification trials into London City Airport.

The programme was subject to some early setbacks large orders from American Eagle and PanAm did not come to fruition so Manx Airlines became the launch customer. Sales were subject to the vagaries of the North American airline market. For example, in 1993 there were only two orders from the USA so BAe organised a world sales tour and performance improvements to drum up orders. As a result, the following year BAe made 53 sales. US airline Atlantic Coast eventually operated 34 J41s and Trans State Airlines flew 27. South African Airlink had 16, British Regional Airlines based in Manchester had a large fleet including 12 J41s and two J31s. This flood of was not sustained and by mid-1995 there was famine forcing the company to cease production in May 1997. In December 1998 BAe delivered its last Jetstream 41 to the Hong Kong Government Flying Service.

BAe leaves the turboprop market

Jetstream 31 customers had been had been clamouring for some years with BAe for a stretched version so by the time the J41 was available they had gone ahead and ordered Saabs and Embraers. The closure of the J41 production line marked the final disentanglement of BAe from its loss-making turboprop business. Production of the J31 ended in 1993 and the 64-seat Jetstream 61 (or ATP) which had been transferred to Prestwick from Woodford was abandoned in 1995. BAe's Commercial Aerospace lost £78m in in 1996. By 1998 British Aerospace's civil aircraft involvement was reduced to the Avro RJ and its 20% share in Airbus.

Following the end of Jetstream production Prestwick built parts for the Nimrod MRA4 and wings for the Avro RJ. In 2006 BAE sold the factory to Spirit Aero Systems which is one of the world's largest Aero structures suppliers for £80m. BAE SYSTEMS Regional Aircraft still has a small facility at Prestwick with around 250 employees. It provides services and solutions to over 650 BAE aircraft in service operated by over 190 customers in 70 countries, i.e., the Jetstream 31/32, Jetstream 41, ATP, HS748 and BAe 146/Avro RJ families.

● The original Astazou engine was the Handley Page design's Achilles' heel. Once BAe Prestwick had refined the design and replaced the engine it proved very successful. The extended Jetstream 41 failed to make similar sales owing to the amount of competition and the volatility of the market.

● With a total of 557 Jetstreams built, credit is due to Handley Page and BAe Prestwick for the airliner's success. Of these 557, 67 Jetstream 1/2/3 were primarily built at Radlett. 386 Jetstream 31s and 32s and 104 Jetstream 41 were constructed, all at Prestwick. Approximately 170 J31/J32s and 64 J41s are still in use. ■

rom September 2016, Jetstream 41 -MAJB is being trialled by HM Coastguard o assess whether fixed-wing aircraft can rovide support for Coastguard Search and Rescue helicopters. *(BAE SYSTEMS)*

Data	Jetstream 31	Jetstream 41
Length	47 ft 2 in	63 ft 2 in
Wingspan	52 ft 0 in	60ft 5in
Height	17 ft 6 in	18ft 10in
MTOW	15,322 lb	24,000lb
Cruising speed	300 mph	340mph
Range	730 mls	891 mls
Crew	2	2
Passengers	19	29/30
Powerplant	2 x 940shp Garret **TPE331**	2×1650shp AlliedSignal TPE33114

The last British airliner – the BAe146

British Aerospace and the 146

At nationalisation in April 1977 the newly formed British Aerospace inherited the Hawker Siddeley 146 jet airliner project which had been given the go-ahead in August 1973 but then a little more than a year later been shelved. However, the unions and workers had protested so fiercely that the Labour Government paid Hawker Siddeley to maintain a small team working on the airliner to allow the nationalised corporation the option of reactivating this project after it was established.

Initial impressions were that the management of the newly-formed British Aerospace also thought the 146 was not viable. Clearly this was not the time for the Unions to relax their pressure. More meetings were held with MPs and the British Aerospace Board. Finally, on 10 July 1978 the Government gave approval for work restart the BAe146.

The BAe 146 goes ahead

The 'resurrected' BAe 146 would be in two forms – a civil airliner and a military cargo lifter - though the cargo lifter was never built. The cost was estimated at £250m, which the newly nationalised firm was

⌃ The BAe 146-100 prototype G-SSSH airborne on its 95-minute maiden flight from Hatfield on 3 September 1981. *(BAE SYSTEMS)*

expected to finance itself. The resurrection of the 146 was part of a BAe strategy to invest in the civil side of the business. The Jetstream 31 was launched and as Hawker Siddeley had remained an Airbus sub-contractor (despite the Labour Government's ill-advised decision to withdraw from it in 1969), BAe was able to buy back into it and become a full risk-sharing partner with a 20% holding.

The BAe 146 was unchanged from the HS146. It had a simple design that could be managed by unsophisticated operators requiring the minimum of ground equipment. The aircraft would have four doors, airstairs, an APU (or batteries) for engine starting, and two freight holds with a low sill height. Two basic versions were on offer in two configurations: the 146-100 seating 70-88

BAe sensibly developed the larger 146-200 at the same time as the 146-100 and it proved to be the best-selling version. The first 146-200, G-WISC was the fourth 146 to fly. It took to the air from Hatfield on 1 August 1982. *(BAE SYSTEMS)*

passengers while the larger 146-200 could seat either 82-102 respectively. Its high wing layout with four Avco Lycoming (later Textron Lycoming) ALF502s provided good airfield performance, which meant that costly features such as leading edge slats and thrust reversers could be omitted on the grounds of weight and complexity. The engines were very quiet and in the years to come this was to be one of the aircraft's major selling points.

Design, final assembly, nose manufacture and flight test of the 146 was centred at the Hatfield plant. Woodford was responsible for the rear fuselage and tail, Filton for the centre fuselage, and wing surfaces, tail and rear fuselage while Textron built the wing in the USA.

Market potential

British Aerospace's analysis of this market was that the 146-100 carrying approximately 85 passengers with its excellent airfield performance could replace the twin turboprop aircraft flying from basic airfields and offer much greater capacity at higher speeds than the existing airliners. These airfields might be situated in remote areas at high altitudes, have challenging obstacle clearance, very short and possibly unprepared runways or, conversely, they might be in city centres where noise would be a critical issue. The larger 146-200 with 100 passengers could replace the larger types where airfield performance was less critical but still important.

The company predicted that the 146-200 would drive older twin jets, such

⌃ The largest version of the 146 design was the 146-300. The first 146 G-SSSH was cut into three and received two fuselage plugs to make it the 146-300 prototype. Re-registered as G-LUXE it is seen here taxiing to a halt after its first flight on the 1 May 1987.
(Derek Ferguson)

➤ Air Wisconsin's 146-200 N2191UE in United Express livery. Air Wisconsin was franchised by United Express to operate regional services.
(BAE SYSTEMS)

as the Boeing 737 or BAC One-Eleven from the skies or require them to have expensive alterations, which would also incur a weight penalty. This analysis proved wrong as airlines fitted 'hush kits' to their aircraft to enable them to meet noise criteria. Later versions of the American types had improved, noise compliant engines.

The total market for the 146 was estimated as more than 1,500 aircraft seating 70-120 passengers and BAe's expectation was that it would sell 400 of the type with breakeven at 250 if the American regional airline market were penetrated - which did happen. The overall sales prediction proved unrealistic, for although almost 400 146/RJs were produced a large proportion of these were leased to airlines, rather than outright sales, and therefore the aircraft continued to be owned by the manufacturer.

The manufacturer rightly expected the average fleet size to be small, from only two aircraft initially, developing to between six and ten. This small fleet size would make selling the 146 challenging and BAe foresaw only a few operators with more than 15 aircraft.

Roll out and first 146-200 order

On 20 May 1981, the day of the 146's roll out, a breakthrough was achieved with a launch order from US regional Air Wisconsin for four 146-200s with options on four more. This order was a benchmark, emphasising the significance of the stretched 200 series, which was to prove the best-selling version of the type. This order stimulated other American carriers; such as Pacific Southwest Airlines (PSA) to follow suit.

The Flight Test Programme

The 146 prototype made high-speed taxi runs and short hops on the evening of 2 September and the next day G-SSSH took to the air at 11:54 from Hatfield's runway 24. It bore the brunt of the test programme and was joined by two more aircraft G-SSHH and G-SSCH in January and April 1982 respectively. The fourth airframe to fly, G-WISC, was the first 146-200 and it flew on 1 August 1982.

The BAe 146 received its CAA Certification on 4 February 1983 after a comparatively short test programme of 1,500 hours flying. It was also the first type certified to the common European Joint Airworthiness Requirements. Four months later, on 20 May the American FAA awarded a type certificate.

Now the BAe 146-300

British Aerospace showed perspicacity with the 146 by launching the 100 and 200 series simultaneously and ensuring that their flight test programmes were completed within three months of each other. The expectation at the time of launch was that the 200 would take just 30% of all sales. Yet when production ended in 2002 the final breakdown of

⌃ The first UK operator of the 146-300 was AirUK. G-UKID later flew with Buzz, CityJet and WDL.
(BAE SYSTEMS)

➤ BAe 146-300, temporarily registered as G-6-191, flying over Hatfield in May 1991. It was delivered to Thai Airways as HS-TBJ. Later it flew with Flybe and Air Libya but was destroyed on the ground in May 2015.
(BAE SYSTEMS)

series production was as follows:
● 47 x 146-100 & RJ70 = 12%
● 203 x 146-200 & RJ85 = 52%
● 142 x 146-300 & RJ100 = 36%

So the decision to produce the 200 series early on was obviously the right one.

The launch of the Fokker 100 in November 1983 was a potential threat to the 146 and Swissair's order for it a few

months later seemed proof of that. The Fokker 100 was a stretched and thoroughly modernised version of the twin-engined F-28 Fellowship jetliner with seating for a maximum of 122 and a modern EFIS glass flightdeck.

To counter the threat of the Fokker 100, BAe announced details of the 146-300 at Farnborough 1984 and said that it would be a 8ft 1in stretch of the 146 yet retaining the same performance as the 200 series. The now privatised British Aerospace's challenge was to raise launch aid from the Government, which only earlier in the year had had to have its arm twisted before granting BAe £250m aid to produce the Airbus A320 wing. Money was also being spent on other projects; the ATP (HS 748 replacement) and on the EAP fighter demonstrator.

Fortuitously, the designers of the bantamweight 100 series gave it a wing of almost Herculean capacity for operation from short, hot and high airfields. Not only did the same wing lift the heavier 200 series with ease, but it could also accommodate the weight of the even heavier 146-300. In 1984, BAe referred to the 300 series as a six-abreast 120-seater, yet by the time the prototype

East-West Airlines 146-300 VH-EWI and 146-200QT VH-JJZ, which although it is in TNT livery was operated by Ansett Air Freight. The former later flew with Flybe and was then scrapped while the QT is now with Star Peru.
(BAE Systems)

took to the air it was promoted in a 100 seat, 32 inch-pitch, five-abreast layout with a 20 inch aisle.

Stretching G-SSSH to make it the 146-300 prototype

Having flown 1,239 hours, G-SSSH made its last flight as a 146-100 on 7 August 1986 and work started almost immediately to convert it into the aerodynamic prototype of the 300 series. The aircraft was cut into three and two fuselage plugs inserted to lengthen the aircraft. Repainted and re-registered as G-LUXE it made its first flight on 1 May 1987.

Pilots found there was virtually no difference in the handling of the 100, 200 or 300 series and certification of the 146-300 was announced on 6 September 1988 at the Farnborough Air Show. If British Aerospace had had any doubts about the wisdom to stretch the aircraft, the announcement of the sale of 19 BAe 146s with the greater majority for the new stretched 300, confounded any criticism.

The 146 in service with major operators

At initial certification in February 1983 the order book had been only 14, with options on 16. Air Wisconsin had taken the lead with the 200 series in the United States while the first British operator was Dan-Air with the 100 series which began services on 27 May 1982 . Other UK operators included Air UK which by the 1990s was the only UK airline employing all three versions of the 146 and another was British European which by the mid-1990s which had a 15 strong 146 fleet.

Air Wisconsin operated the 146-200 and 146-300 until bankruptcy in April 2006. On the West Coast of the USA, the

▲ In addition to the initial 23 QTs (Quiet Traders) built, there were also five QCs (Quiet Convertibles) constructed. These could be converted to passenger carrying in less than 30 minutes. *(BAE Systems)*

aircraft also attracted large orders from Pacific Southwest Airlines and Air Cal but when these airlines were taken over by larger carriers, their 146s were all withdrawn from service.

In 1984 Ansett Group ordered BAe 146-200s and 300s for use by its subsidiaries, Airlines of Western Australia and East-West Airlines. The combined Ansett/TNT group became the largest

customer for the BAe 146 series. Ansett New Zealand flowed suit ordering 146-200s and later eight 300s. Another Antipodean 146 operator, Australian Airlink bought by Qantas in 1992 and was rebranded as Quantaslink. It continued to operate ten 146s but in 2005-6 all of them were replaced.

Chinese Premier Zhao Ziyang visited Hatfield in June 1985 and an order for ten

▲ BAe made substantial efforts to sell a military 146. It developed the Sideloading Tactical Airlifter demonstrator G-BSTA, but none was sold. In April 1990, it flew into Langenlebarn Air Base in Eastern Austria for a demonstration to the Austrian Defence Ministry. *(BAE Systems)*

146-100s was placed as part of a massive re-equipment programme for CAAC supplemented by eight stretched 146-300s delivered between 1992 and 1994. Elsewhere in Asia early users were Thai Airways whose fleet eventually stabilised at five 146-300s used domestic routes from 1982 to 1998, but these were replaced with 737s.

Sssh! The Quiet Trader

The British Aerospace146 is an ideal freighter with its high wing, capacious fuselage floor, proximity to the ground and quietness - so important for much airfreighting which often takes place at night, when airports are promoting their 'good neighbour' policies. Typical freight aircraft are often noisy, gas-guzzling, elderly types, demoted to freight work from passenger flights. The 146-200QT carries up to nine LD3 cargo containers and the 146-300QT ten.

Recognising the QT's versatility for night operation out of noise-sensitive airfields, TNT bought 21 QTs and nine of these QTs remain in operation with ASL Airlines of Spain covering the TNT Express network.

Quiet Convertible

Building on the success of the Quiet Trader a Quiet Convertible (QC) 146 was developed employing the same freight door installation as the QT. The QC is easy to distinguish from the QT, as it has virtually the full complement of windows whereas the QT has none. The QC can be changed from a passenger to an all freight or mixed layout in less than 30 minutes. The QC proved to be an unsatisfactory option, as it was more expensive and heavier than the passenger 146.

QT/QC production and QT programme relaunch 2007

Between 1986 and 1994, 13 146-200QTs, ten 300QT freighters and five 200QCs

▲ The dominance of the 146 at London City has passed but in the 1990s a sight like this was commonplace. 146s and RJs from Malmö, Lufthansa, Alitalia, Crossair and KLM UK.
(BAE Systems)

▼ Swiss RJ100 HB-IYS landing at London City bearing "Shopping Paradise – Zurich" livery. The Swiss RJs are being replaced by Bombardier C-Series twin-jets during 2017.
(Andrew Goldsmith)

were assembled at BAe Woodford. The manufacturer relaunched a QT conversion programme in early 2007. A 146-200 was converted and flew in June 2008 but was broken up for spares. The second conversion, a 146-300 has been leased to Cobham Aviation Services as VH-NJZ. The majority of the QTs and QCs are still in service today and BAE Regional Aircraft is currently proposing a QT version of the RJ.

Military 146s

Military developments of the HS146 had been envisaged from the outset and British Aerospace's relaunch of the 146 in 1978 was predicated on the sale of 100 military rear-loaders but none were ever built. The closest BAe ever got to a dedicated military version was the Sideloading Tactical Airlifter demonstrator, G-BSTA. The second 146 built, a 146-100, was fitted with a freight door like a QT, a 16 seat forward cabin to demonstrate a

military VIP role, a middle cabin demonstrating both the Casevac and Paratroop role and a rear cabin fitted with a roller floor to facilitate pallet loading through the freight door. Despite demonstrations and sales tours, none were sold but the aircraft is still flying as a freighter with Cobham / National Jet Systems in Australia.

The RAF's 146 CC2s

In the early 1980s the Queen's Flight determined to replace its HS 748s with two new BAe 146-100 CC Mk 2s with luxury cabins and wing-root fuel tanks to extend their range to 1,700 miles. The CC2s have three passenger cabins, the most luxurious at the rear, a large bathroom, dressing room and two further cabins forward, a toilet and a large VIP service galley. ZE700 and ZE701 were handed over in April and July 1986 respectively and remain in service. A third 146 CC Mk 2, ZE702 was sold at the end of 2001. In 1995, the Queen's Flight was amalgamated with No 32 Squadron, which had previously operated Ministerial and Military VIP services, and was renamed No 32 (The Royal) Squadron and based at Northolt.

Quiet City

When air services started at London City Airport in 1987 they proved very limited as only the slow turboprop De Havilland Canada Dash 7s operated into there. When the following year the BAe146 entered the equation the prospects for London City Airport began to improve radically. The 146 demonstration at London City Airport in July 1988 proved a great success as the aircraft was able to fly the 5½° approach required and its quietness defied any opposition. The introduction of the BAe 146-200 and 146-300 changed the whole perspective of operation from London City as they were able to quickly and easily reach such major European centres as Copenhagen,

Berlin, Stockholm and Zurich.

Only Swiss and CityJet are still regularly operating Avro RJs into London City at the beginning of 2017 and Swiss is replacing them with more modern types. At one point Dublin-based CityJet had 27 RJ85s and seven of CityJet's RJ85s are due to remain in service for the foreseeable future. The airline focuses on high-frequency services for business travellers including vital linkage routes from major hubs to regional centres in Europe.

Though the predominance of the 146/RJ has passed at London City Airport, the significance of each to the other cannot be under-estimated.

⌃ **The trio of development RJs in September 1992. G-BUFI RJ70, G-ISEE RJ85, and G-OIII RJ100.** *(BAE Systems)*

➤ **Lufthansa operated a fleet of 18 RJ85s from 1994 until 2012.** *(BAE Systems)*

G-6-321 which became N509XJ with Northwest, at one time the largest 146/RJ operator, which received 36 RJ85s between 1997 and 2000. *(BAE Systems)*

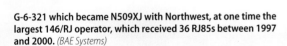

British Aerospace averts bankruptcy

Throughout the late 1980's, British Aerospace needed to generate cash from sales for its large production operation so the number of aircraft on lease had expanded rapidly in the 1980s as the sales force had sought to place the 146s, ATPs and Jetstreams with customers. The manufacturer essentially sold aircraft to finance companies, which then leased them back to BAe for it to remarket them to airlines on short, flexible subleases.

In 1992 the civil market took a dramatic turn for the worse. Airlines began returning significant numbers of their leased aircraft at appreciably depleted values with little prospect of finding new customers at sustainable rates, leaving BAe to pay the lease rentals to the financiers. The impact on profit and cash was disastrous. BAe came close to ruin as it was hit by this financial crisis brought on by the potential financial exposure to its regional aircraft lease book.

The BAe Regional Aircraft business had been driven by the need to fill the factories, rather than delivering valuable business. So with any continuing production there had to be real sales not leases. The objective was to do business with blue chip operators, to go for quality rather than yield - better to take a lower price but get paid in cash.

British Aerospace decided on a

➤

dramatically reduced production rate, down from 42 aircraft a year to 18-20 per year. Production would be limited and market driven not product driven. If BAe could not supply an aircraft quickly that was not to be a problem.

Asset Management
To deal with this large fleet of leased aircraft (which included ATPs and Jetstreams) in January 1993 BAe established the Asset Management Organisation at Bishop Square, Hatfield to manage these aircraft, quite separately from the Sales Organisation. With better planning and more rigorous management they were quickly able to recover and stabilise the situation within a short period.

In January 1993, British Aerospace had 118 BAe 146 aircraft on its books, 21 idle and 40 due to be returned that year. At the peak of the recession there were 44 BAe 146s parked. Within three years, Asset Management had reduced the idle fleet to zero and raised the market value of the lease rates to a level that supported the sales effort of new build aircraft.

Rebranding – Regional Jet
By 1990, with some 202 aircraft ordered and 157 delivered, British Aerospace was satisfied that the 146 had proved a success in competition with the Fokker 100. However, BAe were aware that there was a need to address misgivings amongst some in the airliner market. Just prior to Farnborough 1990 BAe

On 10 January 2002, after cancellation of the Avro RJX, the three RJXs built took to the air for a photo session. The first two RJXs in their element; G-ORJX, RJX85 and G-IRJX, RJX100. The former is in store at BAE Prestwick and the latter made one more flight into nearby Manchester Airport where it is preserved. *(BAE Systems)*

G-LUXE, the 146-100 and later 146-300 prototype, was converted to become an Atmospheric Research Aircraft equipped with a multitude of fuselage-mounted and underwing pod sensors. It can carry a crew of scientists and additional fuel tanks provide a greater range than the standard 146. *(BAE Systems)*

announced a number of major improvements to the 146 family. The most important change to this development of the 146 was the introduction an improved engine, which lowered maintenance costs, which had proved an impediment to some sales. Textron Lycoming added an extra low compressor stage and FADEC which provided smoother running. The LF507 was a great improvement, with a removal rate that was half that of its predecessor.

To emphasise the improvements the aircraft were rebranded as Avro Regional Jets, so each model would be identified by their approximate passenger capacity with five-abreast seating:
- Avro RJ70 (former 146-100)
- Avro RJ85 (former 146-200)
- Avro RJ100 (former 146-300).

As an additional marketing stimulus, the RJs were offered with customer support packages which guaranteed reliability, and maintenance costs would be no higher than a comparable twin-jet.

The RJs in service with major operators
British Aerospace was justifiably pleased that between 1993 and 1995 it had acquired a reputable order book with contracts from four of the six major

European 'blue chip' airlines in the market for regional airliners: Crossair/Swissair, Lufthansa, Sabena and British Airways. These airlines were much more secure than many of the earlier regional operators that had ordered the 146 and whose weaker finances had contributed to BAe's financial problems in 1992.

Swiss formally began operations in April 2002 and it had four Avro RJ85s and 15 RJ100s branded as 'Jumbolinos'. Swiss continues to operate its British jets though they will all be phased out in 2017. In August 2012 Lufthansa said goodbye to the Avro RJ when the last revenue flight arrived at its Munich hub from Cologne flown by RJ85 D-AVRR. In those 18 years, its 18 Avro RJs flew more than 575,000 flights and carried more than 30 million passengers safely to their destinations. At one time in the 2000s Lufthansa had headed up the largest fleet of 146s and RJs which included Lufthansa Cityline, Eurowings, and Air Dolomiti. This made the Lufthansa Regional grouping responsible for the world's largest BAe 146/Avro RJ fleet with 37 aircraft. Now all of those 146s and RJs have been replaced by newer types.

Best-selling British jetliner
With the delivery of D-AVRD to Lufthansa,

Honeywell AS977. It was expected to offer 15% lower fuel burn, 18% better maintenance rates; and lower exhaust noise compared with the LF507 fitted to the RJ. It would provide greater range, lower costs, increased reliability and the ability to operate at higher weights from restricted airports.

The RJX was low-cost, low-risk, high-gain development approach. For BAE Systems to compete most effectively with the newcomers, a switch to a twin-engine configuration would have been necessary but would likely cost $500m, a sum it was unwilling to spend. As in the early 1990s BAE Systems would not finance a major reworking of the design into a twin-engined version as this would require total re-engineering of the wing; a new engine pylon position, increased sweep to increase Mach number and changes to the tail. Such a strategy was not consistent with the company's strategy to only carry out limited improvements to existing aircraft while these were still viable.

Commentators criticised BAE for waiting so long to make this decision, which they had apparently been contemplating since 1998, stating this delay had lost the firm many potential orders. In the latter part of the decade orders had trailed off; from 1994 to 1999 at least 20 RJs had been delivered per year but by 2000 this had fallen to 14 and in 2001 only ten were delivered.

RJX Maiden flight and testing

The first flight of the Avro RJX85 prototype G-ORJX took place Saturday, 28 April 2001, at which time the RJX had orders for 14 aircraft and options on another 14. By August, BAE Systems Regional Aircraft had completed four months of test flying on the new aircraft. The aircraft had a noticeably better performance than the RJ, especially at high altitude. It was joined in the test

BAe's 250th 146/RJ in March 1995 the type had outsold the BAC One-Eleven of which 244 were built. In the previous year, BAe Woodford had delivered 17 RJs, very different to 1991 when the joint production lines at Woodford and Hatfield had produced 39.

The Belgian national airline, Sabena ordered 16 RJ85s and nine RJ100s in September 1995, emulating Crossair by fitting its machines with 82 leather seats in a five abreast layout and Lufthansa followed suit with this luxurious arrangement. Sabena went into liquidation in November 2001, so Brussels Airlines took over its own operations and became SN Brussels. The RJ85s were gradually withdrawn from service in 2011-2014 but the airline continues to lease eight RJ100s. Between 2002 and 2013 BA operated a large fleet of RJs and a small number of 146s flying on domestic and international routes from UK airports and London City.

The Avro RJX and the sudden end of production

The RJ needed development as new competition in the form of the Bombardier CRJ 700/CRJ900 and Brazilian Embraer 170/190 were both gathering large orders, though these suffered after

9/11. In March 2000 BAE Systems formally launched the Avro RJX. The firm had identified that it could revamp the aircraft around an improved powerplant the

The last delivery of a British airliner. RJ85 OH-SAP for Blue 1 together with the prototype 146 and now Atmospheric Research Aircraft G-LUXE at Woodford on 25 November 2003. (BAE Systems)

programme by the first Avro RJX100 G-IRJX on 23 September 2001.

The End

BAE Systems Chief Executive, John Weston made a surprise announcement on 27 November 2001 that the Regional Jet business was no longer viable. At the various BAE sites, 1,669 employees lost their jobs. After cancellation G-ORJX never flew again and in 2011 was transported to BAE Prestwick. G-IRJX was initially stored and then donated to the Manchester Aviation Heritage exhibition, making its last flight into at Manchester Airport on 6 February 2003.

The delivery of the final British-built airliner

The final British-built airliner, an Avro RJ85 OH-SAP was delivered on 26 November 2003 to the Finnish airline Blue 1, bringing to a close 22 years of BAe 146/RJ production. More significantly it the end of a history and tradition of airliner manufacture in Britain, which began with the De Havilland 16 in 1919 and continued with many other firms throughout the ensuing century.

G-LUXE - Atmospheric Research Aircraft

Though RJ85 OH-SAP was the final British airliner delivery, the last civil aircraft delivery from BAe Woodford was on 10 May 2004 when G-LUXE, the original 146-100 prototype and later 146-300 prototype, was handed over to Facility for Airborne Atmospheric Measurements (FAAM) reconfigured as an Atmospheric Research Aircraft.

New roles for the 146/RJ

Though the 146/RJ has been out of production 15 years, BAE SYSTEMS

▲ ZE708 taking off from Broughton following conversion to the RAF C3 configuration. Note the DIRCM defensive sensors and pods under the forward fuselage and aft of the forward door and at the rear. *(BAE Systems)*

continues to promote the aircraft in new roles. Recently it has adopted a new role with the RAF, has become as a trainer for the Empire Test Pilots School, is in use on for Fly in – Fly out operations in Australia and most strikingly has become a Firefighting aircraft in North America.

New role – RAF C3

In 2011 an Urgent Operational Requirement was identified by the RAF to find an aircraft to augment tactical aircraft, during the withdrawal from Afghanistan in 2013-14, transporting people around theatre. In June 2012 BAE Systems was contracted to convert two BAe 146-200QCs to military configuration for the Royal Air Force. Two aircraft were sourced from TNT for the role. BAE Systems Regional Aircraft at Prestwick was responsible for the design and overall management of the programme, with the actual conversion handled by Hawker Beechcraft at Broughton. As the 146 C3s (ZE707, ZE708) were built as 146-200QCs they are equipped with a large 131in x 76in rear upward-opening freight door giving a large aperture for the easy loading of pallets, containers and awkwardly-shaped cargo. The passenger layout of 94 seats is to full commercial aircraft standards.

New role – Test Pilot trainer

In 2011 as a replacement for the Empire Test Pilots' School's two elderly BAC One-Elevens, an Avro RJ70 and Avro RJ100 were acquired by QinetiQ for the ETPS. The RJ70, G-BVRJ is being substantially modified with flight test instrumentation and a ballast transfer system installed for its new role and will become QQ102. The RJ100 was delivered to the ETPS as QQ101 in October 2012.

New role - FIFO – Fly in – Fly out

The 146/RJ has always had a good short take-off and landing performance and in Australia, Cobham has opened-up hundreds of gravel air strips to commercial passenger jet aircraft for the first time, unlocking huge benefits to mining and energy companies for FIFO operations using 82-seat Avro RJ85s equipped with a special protection kit allowing them to land on gravel runways.

The approval follows a project carried out by BAE to increase payload by four tonnes, an additional 700 nautical miles range, or a mix of the two. The aim was to increase the number of passengers that can be carried on Cobham routes from Perth in Western Australia to serve the important mining operations across the vast state.

New role – Firefighter

In a new departure the British jet is carving out a prominent niche in the fire bomber market, as suitably modified examples of the BAe146/Avro RJ85 are well-suited for this demanding role. Three

Cobham's 146-100 VH-NJC equipped with a special 'Unpaved runway protection kit' allowing it to land on gravel runways which is necessary for FIFO 'Fly in, Fly out' support contracts to Australian minerals fields. *(Cobham)*

operators have chosen the BAe 146-200; Minden Air Services, Neptune Aviation Services and Air Spray, while the RJ85 has been chosen by Conair of Canada.

In what turned out to be a very busy 2016 wildfire season in North America, the 14 in-service BAe 146-200s and Avro RJ85s of Neptune Aviation and Conair/ Aero-Flite flew a combined total of well over 5,800 tanker missions, dropping in excess of 12.5 million gallons of retardant to help control some of the 67,595 recorded wildfires in the USA and well over 5,000 in Canada. A further eight BAe 146/Avro RJs are under conversion for this demanding role, with four scheduled to enter service during 2017.

In the USA especially and in many other countries forest fires present a frequent and serious threat to lives and property. In the first half of 2014 more than 1.5m acres of land were burnt to the ground in the USA and the US Government spends $2bn on extinguishing such fires. Where these are in remote areas it may well be that the only way these can be brought under control is with aircraft dropping water, foam, and retardants. Typically the aircraft used for this task were a motley collection of elderly types, but following two crashes in 2002, the US Forestry Service (USFS) cancelled some companies' contracts concentrating minds on the need for more modern equipment. So the providers naturally examined the market for types which would suit the role.

BAE Systems actively engaged with air tanker operators to examine if the BAe146/Avro RJ85, could be sold to them for their ongoing requirements and as a replacement for their ageing fleets. Both the BAe146-200 and RJ85 (of which many more examples are available) are the variants best suited to fit this requirement, as it can carry a 3,000 US gallon tank making it a US Class 1 tanker. The latest USFS contracts require aircraft able to uplift 3,000 US gallons and a minimum cruise speed of 300knots.

Conair and the RJ85

Conair of British Columbia, Canada has been operating for more than 40 years in fighting fires with Airtankers. It is the largest Airtanker operator in the world with approximately 60 aircraft. The relative youth of the airframe and the complete re-engineering of the Avro RJ85 as an Airtanker ensures the aircraft will have sufficient service life to operate safely for up to 25 years as an Airtanker. The Avro RJ85 Airtanker carry a maximum payload of 10,910 litres of fire retardant or water with an endurance of 3.5 hours (including reserves) at a normal cruising speed of 380 knots if required. This provides a high speed Airtanker which is ideally suited to the requirements for prompt dispatch and arrival at the target. With BAE's help Conair decided to install external tanks enveloping the mid-underbelly fuselage while the cabin remains empty. This tank

△ **Conair Tanker 160 N839AC during a fire retardent run. Conair have fitted their RJ85s with external tanks to carry the retardent.** *(Conair)*

contains the fire retardant or water, released through a sophisticated computer-controlled system of doors. Conair now has nine RJ85s in service or being converted as Air tankers.

Conair's RJs have been operational for several years in Canada, the USA and Australia combatting fires. The USFS has contracted Conair in the USA for two RJ85s to be on permanent standby to fight fires for a five-year-period.

Neptune Aviation Services and Air Spray

Neptune at Missoula, Montana uses a conversion of the BAe146-200 equipped with an internal tank also capable of delivering a payload of 3,000 gallons of fire retardant. It now has seven 146-200s active and two under conversion. The latest operator to convert an aircraft is Air Spray of Chico, California, which is in the final stages of converting the first of five BAe 146-200s.

◁ **Neptune Tanker 01 N476NA dropping retardent. Neptune have chosen to use the older 146-200s and are converting them to this role by fitting tanks within the fuselage.** *(Bob Cheatham)*

Conclusion

The BAe 146 / Avro RJ proved to be Britain's most successful jet airliner, though the *turbo-prop* Vickers Viscount outsold it with its total sales of 438 and the Woodford-built Hawker Siddeley 748 turbo-prop almost equalled it with 380 deliveries. ■

Specification	BAe146-200 / Avro RJ85
Length	93ft 8in
Wingspan	86ft 5in
MTOW	92,000lbs/95,000lbs
Max speed	M.073/300kt IAS
Range	1510 nm (RJ)
Passengers	85-100 (5/6 abreast)
Powerplant	Avco Lycoming ALF502R-5 (6,970lb) / Textron Lycoming LF507-1F (7,000lb)

British Aerospace and Airbus

Inception

When British Aerospace was formed in 1977, BAe was not a member of the Airbus consortium but a major sub-contractor designing and building the wings of the Airbus A300. This sub-contract was inherited from Hawker Siddeley Aviation (HSA) whose share of manufacturing amounted to approximately 18% of the A300. From 1966 until 1969 Hawker Siddeley had been a major partner in the tripartite Government-sponsored Airbus project, along with Sud Aviation (later Aerospatiale and now EADS) and

▲Qantas A300 B4 VH-TAA delivered in June 1981. It was later converted to become a freighter. *(Airbus)*

▼YR-LCB was an A310 of TAROM delivered in December 1992. *(Airbus)*

Deutsche Airbus (now EADS) until the British Government withdrew from the project.

Go-ahead

Airbus was instigated as an attempt by the European aircraft industry to wrest domination of the civil airliner market away from the USA. On 26 September 1967, a Memorandum of Understanding on the European Airbus was duly signed in Bonn by the British, French and German Governments. Sud Aviation had overall design leadership for the 300-seater Airbus A300 and in return, Rolls-Royce led

on the engine for the aircraft, the RB207. Britain and France were the major partners providing 37.5% of the costs and sharing work in those proportions, while Germany provided the remaining 25% of the finance and the work. Sud Aviation was to build the flight deck and the fuselage centre section. Hawker Siddeley would build the wing from tip to tip, including the high-lift devices and the engine pylons. The German industry group would build the remainder. Technical direction and final assembly was centred at Toulouse.

Costs escalated and initial estimates were quickly exceeded so all three Governments obliged the Airbus consortium to come up with a cheaper version of their design. At the end of 1968 a new smaller, cheaper 250-seater version of the Airbus was proposed, unimaginatively dubbed the A300B. However, Tony Benn, the British Minister of Technology had become very unenthusiastic towards the project and told his French and German colleagues that the A300B was a new project and that the Memorandum of Understanding on the A300 was dead.

British Government withdrawal

French and German Governmental irritation at the reluctance of the British Government to back the A300B reached a climax in London on 10 April 1969. After a meeting of the three Ministers concerned, the French and Germans announced a

An Airbus montage of the A320 family of airliners. The A321 has the largest capacity and can take up to 230 passengers, the A320's maximum is 195, while the A319 can carry 160. The smallest of the four airliners, the A318, is now out of production. The neo (new engine option) versions of the A320 family are now entering service. *(Airbus)*

decision to proceed alone. They were undeterred by the British withdrawal and indicated that they would proceed in partnership with the development.

From partner to sub-contractor

In June 1969, the Hawker Siddeley Board bravely expressed their firm desire to remain in the European Airbus programme and invest in it privately. France and Germany acknowledged they needed HSA too. Manufacturing the largest wing ever fabricated in quantity in Britain required huge investment and understandably HSA was reluctant to hand over their well-designed Airbus wing to a foreign rival. This left HSA struggling to find a way to recoup the benefits of their extensive contribution of both technical and commercial knowledge in the project and the need for a huge investment in plant and machine tools.

The ramifications of Britain's withdrawal were far-reaching. HSA had previously been contracted to manufacture the whole wing, now production of all the moving parts of the wing, such as the slats, flaps, lift dumpers, etc. was moved to other manufacturers outside the UK. Though HSA was still heavily involved in the project, British withdrawal from the programme was to have long-lasting effects on the British aviation's ancillary industries, since equipment decisions were now made by the French and German partners and the British contribution was much reduced.

Hawker Siddeley became responsible for the largest wings ever then put into production in Europe. Overall control of all wing design and detailing lay with Hatfield, but Broughton manufactured the major part of it.

⌃ An A330 of Virgin Australia, VH-XFC, flying like all other Airbuses on British designed and manufactured wings. The revamped A330neo (new engine option) is due to fly in late 2017. The four-engined version of the A330, the A340 is now out of production. *(Airbus)*

Into the air

The first prototype flew from Toulouse on 28 October 1972 and the second in February the following year. The B1 prototypes were succeeded in the air by two extended fuselage B2s, which were the first production aircraft. Certification followed in March 1974 and scheduled services were started by Air France on the London-Paris route in May providing an exceptionally high degree of reliability and economy. Though FAA certification followed at the end of the month it seemed of little import as there was then no American interest in the aircraft.

The Airbus A300 gradually received orders and though there were no competitors to the Airbus at that time, airlines appeared reluctant to buy an aircraft constructed by a consortium and whether two engines were sufficiently reliable for the carriage of up to 300 passengers. Production continued at a very slow rate and unsold aircraft were parked at Toulouse. To make the aircraft more attractive to potential customers, Airbus developed the A300B4 offering greater range and which was to sell in greater numbers than the B2.

By mid-1976 Hawker Siddeley had orders for 100 wing sets and authorisation to purchase long-lead items for another 32. It had been well worth the risk, as HSA had recouped its investment on delivery of the 25th set of wings.

A RAAF Airbus MRTT (Multi-Role Tanker Transport) refuelling an F-16. The aircraft is based on the A330-200 and its basic fuel capacity is so great that no additional tanks are needed for air-to-air refuelling. *(Airbus)*

British Aerospace becomes a partner of Airbus

At its formation, British Aerospace had a significant if not partnership role in Airbus and was anxious to have a stake in the A300's successor which was soon to be launched. The French and German Governments made approaches to the British Government to rejoin Airbus. A Memorandum of Understanding under which BAe would take a 20% share was signed in December 1977 as a preliminary to re-admittance as a partner. Just as matters seem settled the waters

▼ The first of five Airbus A300-600ST Belugas, F-GSTA which was a heavily rebuilt version of the A300 needed to transport parts of the Airbuses from factory to factory. *(Airbus)*

were muddied when Boeing sought to entice BAe into its embrace as a sub-contractor on the wing of the Boeing 757, powered by Rolls-Royce RB211s and ordered by British Airways which showed no interest in Airbus. Rolls-Royce and some in the Labour Government were pressing for the Boeing-BAe deal while the Europhiles wanted BAe to be a full partner of Airbus, not just a sub-contractor. In the talks between Governments, the French insisted that a condition of British re-admittance was an order by British Airways but the airline

remained intransigent. The French were deeply offended by BA's launch order for the 757.

Eventually a deal was cobbled together whereby BA was permitted to order 757s while the Government announced on 6 November 1978 that BAe would formally join Airbus in January the following year. The Government agreed to financially support BAe's rejoining Airbus as considerable investment in plant would be necessary. It would continue to produce the A300 wings and would have a substantial share in the A310. Freddie Laker ordered ten A300B4s for Laker Airways, becoming the first UK Airbus operator, although BA continued its 'Boeing Always' policy (inherited from BOAC, 'Boeing Only Aircraft Corporation').

Britain, once an equal partner with France in the consortium with Germany, now rejoined in third position with just a 20% holding and without a role for Rolls-Royce. Spain was now a participant, albeit a small player with just a 4.2% share, while France and Germany's share was cut to 37.9% each to accommodate their new partner. This investment by the British Government came with no guarantees of success but following a slow first decade, sales were beginning to accelerate and in 1990 Airbus finally broke even. Some of this success can be attributed to the decision in mid-1978 to proceed with the A310, a medium to long-range 200-seater which had very positive impact on sales figures.

After much political manoeuvring, Britain at last secured for itself the design and production of the A310 wing. British Aerospace, with first-hand experience of the A300, was the logical choice for the new wing, but had to compete strongly with a German-design for the work. Once again design of the A310 wing was BAe Hatfield's responsibility, while Broughton built them. The 210-seat A310 was essentially a shorter-fuselage version of the A300, but with a new wing, modified engines and improved technology such as a digital flight control system. The new wing was a key feature of the aircraft, providing competitive performance through significant aerodynamic and structural improvements. The A310 proved to be moderately successful and production only ceased in 1998 after 255 had been manufactured.

The A320 – final assembly or wing contract?

Airbus's first two airliners, the A300 and A310 received very respectable sales but the next Airbus was a game changer. Meanwhile in mid-1977 BAe also joined the JET (Joint European Transport) consortium to build a 130-170 seater and in return for funding 30-35% of it, the Government wanted design leadership and final assembly. The French would not accept these stipulations, seeing JET as an Airbus project and would not negotiate on design leadership or final assembly.

In 1979 the JET project (which

⌃ **A Beluga being loaded with Airbus A340-600 wings at the Airbus Broughton site.** *(Airbus)*

became the A320) moved from Weybridge to Toulouse when BAe joined Airbus. Some on the BAe Board wanted the company to bid to undertake A320 final assembly at Filton but this would have required a 30% financial stake in the project and heavy investment in plant and equipment. BAe won manufacture of

the entire wing, unlike the A300 and A310 where the moving surfaces were built elsewhere. The wing design originated from the Weybridge plant rather than Hatfield but manufacture was centred at Broughton. After intense lobbying of the Prime Minister, Margaret Thatcher and very much against the

⌃ **Until 2006 the Airbus factories in the UK were owned by BAE. Wings for the A380 are designed and built at Airbus's two sites in the UK, Filton, near Bristol and Broughton, North Wales. In Broughton, an 83,500 square metre (over 900,000 sq ft) facility was built to house wing assembly for the A380 as well as other aircraft manufacturing activity.** *(Airbus)*

views of Norman Tebbit, the Secretary of State for Industry, BAe managed to wrest £250m from the Government, which was to be recouped by a levy on sales. This sum was not the total amount needed as BAe had to invest some £200m of its own for the project. To have gone ahead with the earlier idea of final assembly and flight testing of the A320s at Filton would have required additional investment of £100m (at 1983 prices).

The A320, which finally went ahead in March 1984, tackled the dominance of the twenty-year-older Boeing 737 design head-on by innovation - introducing 'Fly by wire' and sidesticks instead of the conventional flying controls to the flightdeck of a civil aircraft. These innovations stole a march on Boeing's capabilities, attracting huge airline and media interest. There was no mechanical connection between the sidestick and the flying surfaces and the Flight Management System maintains the aircraft within its envelope, necessarily limiting angle of attack, airspeed and deflection of flight controls. If the pilot keeps the aircraft within the envelope there is no intervention in control.

In December 2016, the A320 family with the larger A321, the progressively smaller A319 and A318 and improved A320neo (new engine option) have achieved more than 12,400 sales with a backlog of more than 5,500. It is produced at Toulouse, Hamburg, Tianjin in China and Mobile, Alabama. Production rates are planned to reach 60 per month, all aircraft flying on British-made wings. The A320 family has proved itself as a most successful competitor to the world's best-selling airliner, the Boeing 737.

Airbus continued to expand its portfolio of types with the A330/340 and for all its success required huge investment funded in part by Government loans and in May 1987, the UK Government provided BAe with a £450 million loan towards its participation in the A330/A340 programme. The A330 was a large capacity, twin-aisle, medium-range, twin-engined airliner while the four-engined A340 was the long and ultra-long-range version. The aircraft shared the same fuselage and the same wing, the most significant difference was the number of powerplant. Fuselage lengths of the A330 and A340 varied as the types were developed. (Though the A330 is still in production and the re-engined, improved A330neo is to fly in 2017, production of the A340 ended 2012.) BAe called on Government support for the A330/A340 and in May 1987 the Conservative Government agreed a £450m loan to BAe for its continuing involvement in Airbus.

With Hatfield's closure, BAe Filton took over overall design responsibility for the A330/A340 wing while Broughton continued to build them. The first A340 wings were completed in June 1990, the first A330 wings in August 1991 and were

then transported to Bremen for completion. In March 2000, the UK was the first Government to invest in the huge A380 when it offered £530m to be repaid over 17 years to safeguard wing manufacture at Filton and Broughton. By January 2006 over 4,000 Airbus wing sets had been manufactured at Broughton. Initially Airbus wings had been flown out of Manchester Airport and after

⌄ The huge British-built wing of the A380 flexing under the weight of its engines. (Airbus)

lengthening of Broughton's runways could be flown from there by Airbus Beluga freighters, but owing to their size the A380 wings could only be moved by road and sea. The A380 flew in April 2005 and after a multitude of problems involving the electrical wiring entered service in October 2007, but by that time BAE Systems was no longer an Airbus partner.

Data	Airbus A320
Length	123ft 3in
Wingspan	117ft 5in
Height	38ft 7in
MTOW	172,000lbs
Max speed	M 0.78 / 541mph
Range	3,300nm (normal payload)
Passengers	190-195
Powerplant	CFM56 27,000lbs / Pratt & Whitney V2500 27,000lbs

◄ The first of 40 Airbus A300B4 Freighters converted by BAe Aviation Services at Filton flew on 23 January, 1997. It was delivered to Channel Express on 19 July 1997. *(BAE SYSTEMS)*

BAE Systems sells its 20% holding in Airbus

In 1998-9, Germany and the UK were close to a pan-aerospace tie-up that would have left France's industry as the minority partner in Airbus, but then BAe decided to buy the UK's Marconi Electronic Systems, ending prospects of a tie-up with DASA. This left Germany (which had acquired Spain's CASA) and France ready to move closer as the newly created BAE SYSTEMS focused on its defence and systems integration businesses.

DASA did not want to be swallowed up by the new BAE SYSTEMS and bought CASA of Spain and then merged with Aérospatiale, coming together as EADS (European Aeronautic Defence and Space Company). The result was that EADS now had an 80% holding in Airbus and BAE SYSTEMS just 20%, not a position from which it could exert much influence. Immediately BAE had to deny rumours that it had any intention of withdrawing from Airbus. However BAE enjoyed the sizeable revenue and profits that its Airbus activities generated, and was fully behind the 1999-2000 revamp of the original consortium structure into an integrated company as it prepared to create the world's largest airliner, the A380. No longer would BAE staff and plants supply parts to another Airbus partner instead, all the Airbus operations across Europe were merged into one, with BAE holding a 20% stake in the company that ran them.

In 2006 the BAE Board decided to sell its share and concentrate its activities on Defence market. Despite early Stock Market expectations of BAE raising £2.2bn from this sale of its stake to EADS, Airbus was hit by major problems with the A380 and its share price dropped sharply, so BAE SYSTEMS only realised £1.87bn but this allowed it to invest more in the US market. BAE's share price rose strongly on the Stock Market though some commentators took a contrary view and felt the sale was a dubious move and wondered why the Government had not intervened.

Despite BAE's withdrawal from Airbus and total disengagement from the civil airliner market, the UK Government continued to recognise the importance of Airbus and invested £340 million in the Airbus A350 programme. The UK's workshare on the A350 has declined from previous Airbuses and amounts to only 18% of the total on the type. Airbus UK

▲ From 1993 to 2002 BAe Aviation Services Filton undertook heavy maintenance on all Airbus types and carried out freighter conversions on A300B4s. Here are A300s of Apollo, Air India and Translift in the Brabazon hangar. *(BAE SYSTEMS)*

remains well-established at Filton and Broughton continuing to manufacture wings for the A320 family, A330, A350, A380 and A400M military freighter.

BAe Aviation Services - Airbus maintenance and freighter conversion programme

BAe Aviation Services was formed at Filton as an MRO, (maintenance, repair and overhaul organisation) in 1993 after the lucrative F-111 relifing contract had ended and VC10 K4 tanker work had passed its peak. It undertook heavy maintenance work on all Airbuses and passenger to freighter conversions on Airbus A300 B4s. Besides the freighter conversions Aviation Services won contracts for Airbus maintenance with Continental, Indian Airways, Egyptair, Qantas, Monarch, Virgin and other airlines.

The decision by BAe to launch its own conversion programme for the A300 in 1996 was made despite conversions being available within the Airbus through Daimler-Benz Aerospace Airbus, which has been installing Airbus cargo doors since 1979. What BAe did was introduce competition to the market and undercut the German conversion price. The increasing availability of used A300 airframes helped the market for the widebody freighter to evolve.

The first Airbus A300B4 freighter conversion flew on 23 January, 1997. This aircraft, originally delivered to Eastern Airlines in 1980 was destined for UK cargo airline, Channel Express. C-S Aviation Services, an aircraft lessor, which ordered eleven conversions from BAe, placed the next two ex-Air France A300B4-200s freighter conversions with HeavyLift Cargo Airlines. Fitted with a 3.58m x 2.56m freight door and cargo handling system and interior, these aircraft had an 85,000 - 95,000lb payload and 2,100 nm range. In all 40 A300B Freighters conversions were made and amongst the other customers were DHL, MNG, TACA, Jet Link, Tradewinds and TNT.

In aftermath of 9/11 in May 2002 BAE sought a buyer for Aviation Services at Filton, citing the lack of a sustainable orderbook, so much so that some A300s stored a Filton were scrapped. Flight Structures of Arlington near Seattle, Washington purchased the Airbus A300 passenger-to-freighter conversion line and Aviation Services was run down. ■

Harrier
conquering the vertical

△XP836 and XP831, the second and first P1127 prototypes respectively. XP836 has the experimental high-speed engine lips and XP831 which is lacking undercarriage doors and other fittings has the standard intakes. XP836 crashed when one of the engine exhaust nozzles detached in flight. *(Hawker Archive)*

By the late 1970s when British Aerospace came into being, the Harrier was well-established in service with the RAF, the US Marines and in production for the Spanish and Royal Navies.

The first prototype P1127 and the forerunner of the Harrier XP831 had made its first tethered hover on 21 October 1960. A lengthy development programme began, with six aircraft assigned to prove the concept. The test programme painstakingly evaluated the performance of the aircraft in horizontal and vertical flight and gradually approached the complexities of a smooth transition between the two. Naturally when developing a new concept there were many challenges, such as an optimum engine intake shape for both hovering and high speed flight. Another was refining the operation of the reaction controls at the wing tips, nose and tail and at the wing tips during hovering to provide directional, attitude and roll control. There were flight test crashes during the test programme but fortunately no fatalities.

In 1961 the United States funded development of the airframe and engine on condition a tripartite (UK/US/German) operational evaluation unit was formed which was equipped with nine additional

▼ XS694, one of the nine Kestrels built for the Tripartite Squadron showing how the aircraft could be dispersed in the event of conflict.
(Hawker Archive)

aircraft known as Kestrels. The unit was formed in October 1964 and its aircraft flew 1,200 sorties until the completion of evaluation flying in November 1965.

Early Harriers with the RAF
In the wake of 1965 defence cuts and the cancellation of the supersonic P1154 V/STOL development of the P1127, the UK ordered a military version of the P1127, which was officially named the Harrier in 1967. The Harrier GR1 was equipped with twin 30mm Aden guns and had the ability to carry a wide variety of stores on five external pylons.

The Harrier GR1s joined No 1 Sqn at Wittering and three squadrons with RAF Germany, only three years after the first development aircraft flew. The RAF also received 13 T2s, twin-seaters which retained full operational capability. An additional squadron of Harriers was soon ordered for the Royal Air Force bringing total orders for this aircraft, (including the US Marines' order) close to 200. The RAF found themselves in possession of a uniquely flexible aircraft, which could be dispersed close to the troops and provide

Following the order for the Harrier by the RAF, six Development Batch Harriers XV276 - XV281 flew in 1966-67. The six aircraft, some unpainted, are shown at Dunsfold at a Press Day for the RAF Harrier with XV280 at the front. *(Hawker Archive)*

quick and effective response to incursions.

Most of the GR1s were fitted with the more powerful Pegasus 10 offering another 1,000lbs thrust, becoming GR1As. They were modified into GR3s, with a nose extension to accommodate a LRMTS (Laser Ranger and Marked Target Seeker) and a RWR (Radar Warning Receiver) fairing on the tail. These converted aircraft were reinforced by 40 new-build Harrier GR3s which received the Pegasus 11 with another 1,000lbs thrust. Happily, these ongoing modifications kept the work flowing at both the Kingston and Dunsfold factories.

Six Harrier GR1As were sent to Belize to deter the aggressive intentions of neighbouring Guatemala in November 1975, in their first out-of-theatre operational deployment. As they were not granted landing rights in the USA they were supported by Victor tankers and flew via Goose Bay and Bermuda. They were withdrawn in April 1976, but the threat resurfaced in July 1977 and so Harriers remained based in Belize until 1993.

Harriers twin-seater

With the development of the RAF GR1 there was a pressing need for a twin-seater and with more engine power available the Harrier T2 was devised. A tandem cockpit within a lengthened fuselage accommodated the trainee pilot. The front cockpit had to match the GR1 while the rear had to give the instructor full authority over all controls.

Deliveries of Harrier T2s began to the

➤ Three Harrier GR3s. Many Harrier GR1s were were modified into GR3s, with a nose extension to accommodate a LRMTS (Laser Ranger and Marked Target Seeker) and a RWR (Radar Warning Receiver) fairing on the tail. *(Hawker Archive)*

Harrier Conversion Unit at Wittering in July 1970. Further trials took place in the meantime so that the Harrier Trainer could carry the full range of stores. More Pegasus power meant that the T2 soon became the T2A. Further developments then followed to keep pace with the RAF's single-seaters, for example the T4 becoming the trainer for the GR3.

In 1970 HSA decided to build a company-owned demonstrator, estimating that it would more than pay for itself in sales. Registered G-VTOL, it flew on 16 September 1971 and appeared in countless demonstrations around the world operating on land and from carriers. This great example of the type has been preserved at the Brooklands Museum.

The American Marines and the Harrier

The purchase of 12 Hawker Siddeley Harriers for the US Marine Corps in December 1969 was the first export order for the Harrier and its significance cannot be underestimated. Altogether 102 single-seater AV-8A and eight TAV-8A twin-seaters were manufactured at HSA plants in the UK. The USMC Harriers were designated AV-8A (the two initial letters standing for Attack, V/STOL).

Hawker Siddeley entered into a co-operative production agreement with McDonnell Douglas of St Louis, Missouri, for the licensed manufacture of subsequent aircraft in America. They were virtually identical to the RAF aircraft, except

Hawker Siddeley built a Harrier trainer as a company demonstrator, appropriately registered G-VTOL. It is seen here flying over Rio, Brazil, carrying large underwing drop tanks. *(Hawker Archive)*

for the powerplant which was the uprated Pegasus 11 of 22,500lb in place of the 19,500lb Pegasus 6.

This connection between HSA (later BAe) and McDonnell Douglas was to have major ramifications for the history and development of the Harrier, as jointly-funded work progressed to define an advanced version of the Harrier embodying a more powerful engine.

The Spanish Navy bought six AV-8As and two TAV-8As Harriers after a Harrier demonstration by test pilot John Farley on Spain's aircraft carrier. In 1977 an additional five aircraft were ordered. Those remaining serviceable were sold to Royal Thai Navy in 1996 where they had only a limited life.

Sea Harriers for the Royal Navy and the Indian Navy

In 1971 the Royal Navy issued a requirement for a fighter, reconnaissance, and strike aircraft for operation from the

▼ A US Marine Corps AV-8A Harrier, assigned to VMA-231. *(Hawker Archive)*

new small *Invincible* class vessels and 24 Sea Harrier FRS1s were ordered for the Royal Navy in 1975. Despite both the US Marine Corps and the Spanish Navy operating their AV-8s from aircraft carriers, this was the first truly navalised version of the Harrier.

The most prominent changes introduced into the Naval version was the raised cockpit to give the pilot a better rearward view so necessary in combat and the fitting of a nose-mounted radar. Invisible from the outside were improvements to the attack avionics and systems.

XZ438, the FRS1 first flew in August, 1978, and in November the first Sea Harrier carrier landing took place aboard HMS *Hermes*. The invention of the Ski-jump gave the aircraft extra lift on take-off, increasing payload that could be carried. The Sea Harrier and the 'Ski jump' were simultaneously introduced on the carriers

and proved their efficacy during the Falklands War. Including replacements for aircraft lost in the Falklands War, a total of 61 Sea Harrier FRS1s and two-seat T4Ns were purchased for the Royal Navy Fleet Air Arm.

In 1978 the Indian Navy became the only other buyer of the Sea Harrier and placed an initial order for six FRS51s and two T60s to operate from the *Vikrant*. In 1986 India bought Britain's ski-jump-equipped *Hermes* for service and renamed it the *Viraat*. India bought a total of 23 Sea Harrier FRS51s and four T60 trainers, to equip its two vessels. The first FRS51 delivery was in December 1983 and were operational until March 2016.

'Mission impossible without V/STOL'

Without the Navy's two carriers and 800 and 801 Sea Harrier squadrons it is highly unlikely that *Operation Corporate*, the 75-day war to recover the Falklands Islands from Argentinean aggression in 1982 would have been successful. The UK's forces were faced with an immense task as the nearest base was Ascension Island, 4,000 mls distant. The Sea Harriers concentrated its aircraft on air defence, engaging enemy Canberras, Daggers (an Israeli version of the Mirage) and Skyhawks. Two of Sea Harriers were lost to enemy action and two collided in mid-air.

As the war progressed No 1 Sqn RAF Harrier GR3s were readied for action in the South Atlantic. BAe Kingston was heavily involved with the MoD establishing alterations for aircraft carrier operation, major improvements to avionics and kits to facilitate Sidewinder missile operation and install Chaff dispensers. Meantime the crews were frantically training; on Yeovilton's Ski jump, with weapons practice and interceptions with French Air Force Mirages and Super Etendards, aircraft types they might engage with during hostilities.

For No 1 Squadron's Harriers to reach the fleet, they had to make a record tanker-supported transit to Ascension Island and join the *Atlantic Conveyor*, a merchant vessel requisitioned to transport the aircraft and helicopters to the proximity of the aircraft carriers. When they reached them, the RAF's Harriers flew on to the *Hermes*. On missions the RAF Harriers endured withering ground fire and missiles as they engaged in close support. They proved their worth, shooting down helicopters, bombing airfields, attacking Argentine ground stores, and reconnaissance.

In all 28 Sea Harriers FRS1s and 14 Harrier GR3s took part in Operation Corporate. Altogether three of the original No 1 Sqn aircraft were lost through enemy action during 125 sorties, all thankfully without loss of life. Their attrition was far higher than the Sea Harriers which lost only two from enemy action during 2,197 sorties and reflected the danger of close support operations in contrast with the Sea Harriers' air superiority role. Clearly without the Harrier the Falklands Islands would not have been regained.

Sea Harrier 2

In December 1988 the UK Ministry of Defence contracted British Aerospace to upgrade the Royal Navy's Sea Harriers with new radars, avionics, and weapons. The

▲ The Spanish Navy received six AV-8A and two TAV-8A Harriers. Here one of the TAV-8As is seen on a 'Ski Jump'. *(Hawker Archive)*

The first production Royal Navy Sea Harrier FRS1 XZ450 made its maiden flight at Dunsfold on 20 August 1978. It was retained for development flying but with the onset of Falkland Islands conflict it was called into service and was shot down over Goose Green. *(Hawker Archive)*

Return in triumph after the Falklands conflict. *HMS Hermes* entering Portsmouth with Harriers, Sea Kings and Pumas on the deck. *(Hawker Archive)*

contract covered modification of all RN FRS1s to FRS2 standard. These were later joined by 18 newly built aircraft, making a total of 60 FRS2s.

The original Blue Fox radar was replaced by the Blue Vixen radar needed for the AIM-120 AMRAAM (Advanced Medium-Range Air-to Air Missiles) and fitted into an enlarged and lengthened nose. The weapons portfolio included Sea Eagle anti-ship and Alarm anti-radiation missiles. A longer rear fuselage was constructed providing extra space for an avionics bay. The Sea Harrier FRS2 had four wing pylons and a centreline station, and the underbelly strakes could be replaced by gun packs or a pair of AIM-120 pylons.

The FRS2 conversion work took place at Kingston and at the Dunsfold flight test centre, supported by Brough. The first production FRS2, XZ497 flew in June 1991 and the first deliveries were made to the Fleet Air Arm in mid-1994. The Sea Harriers FRS2 did not remain in service for long as they were withdrawn in 2006. Altogether the Sea Harrier served served the Navy for 25 years.

The alternative Harrier 2 developments

Under their 15-year agreement made in 1969, both HSA Kingston and McDonnell Douglas collaborated on further developments of the Harrier. In the early 1970s they proposed the AV-16 Advanced Harrier and a supersonic version for the UK, an AV-16S, the aim of which was to double

the AV-8's payload and range capabilities. Owing to British Government concerns about the cost and the small 60 aircraft requirement for the RAF, the UK withdrew from the project in 1975 and ceased to be a partner of McDonnell Douglas. This withdrawal caused ructions in the UK where Britain was seen to be handing over its unique V/STOL heritage concept to the USA.

HSA and McDonnell Douglas then independently projected different future developments of the Harrier. HSA proposed the GR5(K) and McDonnell Douglas the AV-8B. The AV-8B had a larger, composite wing, LERX (Leading Edge Extensions), lift refinements and raised cockpit. McDonnell Douglas began development of the AV-8B in 1975 and the first of two YAV-8B prototypes; modified AV-8As flew in November 1978 to prove the modifications. The changes doubled the AV-8's payload/range performance. Meanwhile Kingston worked on a larger metal wing Harrier with six to eight pylons and wingtip missile rails. To the manufacturer's disappointment the British Conservative Government did not support the Harrier GR5(K) and Britain's V/STOL technology.

BAe becomes a sub-contractor on the Harrier AV-8B

Hawker Siddeley/BAe had hoped that the McDonnell Douglas version would not been funded and then directly sell its own Harrier development to the USMC. Without British Government support that could not

⌃ **Two US Marine Corps Harrier AV-8Bs on a USMC amphibious assault ship.** *(Hawker Archive)*

Sea Harrier FRS2 ZH809 and a T8. Delivered in 1998, the bright blue ZH809 was withdrawn from service in 2006 having flown just 1,073 hours. The aircraft had a special paint scheme applied for the 2004 display season. *(Hawker Archive)*

▲ A Spanish Navy AV-8B landing on the Spanish Navy's aircraft carrier *Príncipe de Asturias*. *(Hawker Archive)*

happen. In August 1981 a Memorandum of Understanding was signed by the US and UK Governments whereby British Aerospace became a sub-contractor to McDonnell Douglas building 40% of the aircraft while Rolls-Royce produced 75% of the engine with Pratt & Whitney building 25%. McDonnell Douglas and British Aerospace signed a joint manufacturing agreement to build 390 Harrier 2s, 328 AV-8Bs for the USMC and 62 Harrier GR5s for the RAF.

The USMC's first AV-8B entered service in August 1985. The first UK GR5

Development aircraft ZD318 flew at Dunsfold on 30 April 1985. The initial UK order was boosted in April 1988 with a follow-on order for 34 Harrier 2s, designated as Harrier GR7s and fitted with night-attack avionics and an electronic countermeasures system. The GR5s were subsequently brought up to GR7 standard. The RAF aircraft were similar to the AV-8B but had numerous differences including eight rather than six pylons to allow for the carriage of Sidewinder missiles, twin Aden cannon, a Martin-Baker ejection seat and different avionics. The T10 trainer had a full operational capacity.

UK Harrier production ended with the GR9 and its trainer, the T12 which were upgrades of the GR7 and T10. These had a new rear fuselage, an upgraded Pegasus 107 offering 24,750lbs thrust (almost 3,000lbs more than GR7) and 100% LERX (Leading Edge Root Extension) in contrast to the 65% extension on the GR7. These improvements had a marked effect on the aircraft's performance as did the further refinements to its avionics and weapons capabilities. The first conversion, ZD230 flew from Warton on 30 May 2003.

Spanish and Italian Navy Harrier

The Spanish Navy's twelve EAV-8B Matadors first deliveries were in October 1987 and operated from Ski-jump-equipped Spanish Navy carrier *Príncipe de Asturias*. During 1993 the Spanish aircraft were in action in 'Operation Deny Flight' over Bosnia and Herzegovina. In 2003 its EAV-8Bs were modified by Boeing (which took over McDonnell Douglas in 1997) to become EAV-8B Plus Matadors.

The Italian Navy considered both the Sea Harrier and the AV-8B for their use and in 1989 chose the Harrier 2, placing an order for 16 AV-8Bs and two TAV-8Bs. The first three AV-8Bs and the two TAV-8Bs were assembled in the USA and the remainder were assembled in Italy. The Italian Harriers saw action from the aircraft carrier *Garibaldi* in the attack on Afghanistan in 2001-2 and were also deployed supporting the military intervention in Libya in 2011.

▲ A RAF Harrier GR5 at Dunsfold. Note its eight underwing pylons and under-fuselage strakes which could be replaced by 30mm cannon. *(Hawker Archive)*

Harrier 2s in USMC and RAF service

During US offensive operations in Kuwait in 1991, 'Operation Desert Storm', the Marine Corps Harrier 2s demonstrated the Harrier's ability to operate from forward bases, from a gravel runway only 100mls from the Kuwaiti border, which traditional fixed-wing aircraft could not do. The 66-stong Harrier fleet flew over 3,000 sorties and dropped almost 3,000 tons of ordnance. The USMC Harriers 2s were also heavily employed in 'Operation Iraqi Freedom' in 2003 where they were more than 40% of the Marines attack force and were based on four assault ships on the Arabian Gulf. A small fleet of USMC Harrier 2s took part in the bombing of Yugoslavia and in 2011 in the bombing of Libya during the operation to overthrow Colonel Gaddafi. More recently they were in regular use in Afghanistan.

The RAF's GR7s first combat use was in Operation Deliberate Force, the UN campaign over Bosnia in 1995. They flew close air support missions, supporting ground troops, carried out reconnaissance and strike missions inside during the Iraq War in 2003. The RAF's Harriers served in Afghanistan from 2004 until 2009; over five years of continuous operations and flew over 22,000 hours in 8,500 sorties.

Merging the RN and RAF fleets

In the 1998 Defence Review the RN Sea Harriers and the RAF Harriers were merged into a single joint command - yet full integration was impracticable as the two types had less than 20% airframe and avionics commonality. The Review concluded that upgrading the Sea Harriers was not viable so the GR7s were upgraded to GR9 standard and were issued to two Fleet Air Arm squadrons as well as to the

Three RAF Harrier T10s, the trainer version for the Harrier GR5. *(Hawker Archive)*

The GR5 and GR7 Harriers were externally very similar, with most of the differences being 'under the skin'. External differences include the FLIR mount on the upper surface of the GR7's nose, plus the latter also had Zeus 'horns' underneath the nose. *(Hawker Archive)*

RAF while the Sea Harriers were retired. This resulted in the RN retaining fast jet expertise and the carriers having greatly enhanced offensive strike capability.

In the 2010 Strategic Defence Review the Harriers and the aircraft carriers were scrapped. The Harrier GR9s were sold for spares to the US Marines.

Harrier production

The P1127s and Kestrels were constructed at Kingston, assembled and flown from Dunsfold. Following the development of the Harrier for the RAF, Kingston built the forward fuselage and Brough the rear fuselage, taking over wing assembly from Hamble in 1969. Dunsfold continued to retain its role as the centre for final assembly and flight test. With the closure of the factory at Kingston in 1992, Harrier forward fuselage production was passed to Dunsfold which closed when production of new-build Harriers ended in 2000. With the completion at Brough of the final rear fuselages for the GR9 upgrade in 2007, British manufacture of the Harrier came to an end after 48 years.

Conclusion

The Harrier was in the right place at the

Data	Harrier GR9
Length	46ft 4in
Wingspan	30 ft 4in
Height	11ft 8in
MTOW	31,000 lbs (Short take off)
Max speed	662 mph at sea level
Combat range	380 mls
Crew	1
Engine	Rolls-Royce Pegasus 105 21,750 lb thrust
Armament	Guns 2 x 25mm Aden cannon Missiles: Sidewinders, Maverick Bombs: unguided 1,000lb, Laser-guided. Also Drop tanks, Reconnaissance pod

▼ **No 1 (F) Squadron RAF Harrier GR9s at Cottesmore.**
(BAE SYSTEMS)

right time. Harrier operations during the Falklands War confounded the critics of many air forces who thought it would shot out of the skies by the supersonic Mirage. Despite this demonstration of its abilities its export potential was never truly achieved, as many air forces had long runways and still sought truly supersonic aircraft.

If Britain alone had been involved in the aircraft's development, then sales would have been comparatively limited and the Harrier 2 would probably not have existed. The US Marine Corp order and the resulting co-operation with McDonnell Douglas led to greater development than would have otherwise been the case. However, in the process the Americans became the leaders in the aircraft's development.

The Harrier proved a highly profitable investment for Hawker Siddeley/BAe provided large export earnings for the UK. Sad to say, the Harrier no longer graces British skies but it does fly with the USMC and the Italian and Spanish Navies. ■

Nimrod - from success to cancellation

When British Aerospace came into being in 1977 the 38 Nimrod MR1s and three R1s were already bedded down in service with the RAF. The MR1s had replaced the ancient Shackletons in the RAF Maritime Reconnaissance role and the R1s though outwardly similar were especially developed versions for electronic reconnaissance and took over from three Comet 2Rs. Whereas the Nimrod MR1s, MR2s and the R1s all put in years of invaluable service, the two succeeding marks though developed and costing billions, never entered service but were ignominiously and controversially scrapped.

The Nimrod design was based on a Comet 4 airframe with the wing centre section enlarged to take four Rolls-Royce Spey 250s instead of Avons. An unpressurised pannier fitted under the pressurised fuselage provided a 48ft long weapons and equipment bay and a large nose radome, to allow for existing and future radar scanners. The large

The final Comet on the production line was rebuilt as the first Nimrod prototype at Broughton and made its first flight to Woodford on 23 May 1967. Note the large number of cabin windows which differentiated it from the production Nimrods. The MAD tail boom is not fitted in this photo as an anti-spin parachute was installed in its place.
(Avro Heritage)

weapons bay could carry of a variety of weapons; bombs, torpedoes and depth charges - alternatively house air-sea rescue gear, or long-range fuel tanks for global ferrying, or freight panniers. Owing to the increased side area, a prominent dorsal fin was fitted and an Electronic Counter Measures fairing at the top of the fin. To make the aircraft even more distinctive there was a Magnetic Anomaly Detector mounted in a long tail boom.

The pilots' windscreens were deepened to confer better visibility during search, and two eyebrow windows added to enable the crew to look into the turn when the aircraft was banked during manoeuvres at low altitude. In addition, two underwing pylons were introduced for external stores and a trainable 70 million candlepower searchlight was installed in the front of starboard external wing tank.

The Rolls-Royce Spey 250 was rated at 11,500lb and thrust reversers were fitted on the outboard tailpipes. The Nimrod could climb quickly to a transit altitude of 30,000ft and cruise at 400kt, descending to search altitude and shutting-down the outboard engines as required. For low-level searches, two engines were kept running at a fairly high thrust level to retain a low specific consumption. The aircraft could climb on one engine at normal search weights and on two engines at maximum weight. The crew numbered 11 consisting of two pilots, one flight engineer, two lookouts, a routine navigator, a tactical navigator, a radio operator, an ASV radar operator and two sonar operators.

Flight test

As there were two Comet 4Cs remaining unsold on the Broughton production these were reworked as Nimrod prototypes. The first Nimrod prototype XV148 flew on 23 May 1967 from Broughton to Woodford and the second, XV147 from Woodford on 31 July 1967. XV148 was rebuilt with Spey engines, however as it would have been a more costly task to rebuild XV147 with Speys it retained its Rolls-Royce Avons.

The Nimrod in service

The Nimrod MR1 entered service in July 1970. Following on from the 38 Nimrod MR1s on the HSA Woodford production were three Nimrod R1s, XW664, 65 and 666. They were delivered to RAF Wyton where they were fitted with their equipment and operational flying only began in May 1974. They had no MAD tail and were considerably different internally

▲ First production Nimrod MR1 XV226 which flew over 400 hours on manufacturers and service trials. *(Avro Heritage)*

as the aircraft carried a large variety of electronic listening and recording equipment. Owing to the increasing complexity and demand for electronic intelligence these aircraft were frequently updated with new and additional equipment, stored in the fuselage and within the large under-fuselage structure. As more equipment was needed the number of crew burgeoned.

The Nimrods MR1s were not long in service before they were upgraded to MR2s by replacing their ASV radar inherited from the Shackleton with the Thorn-EMI Searchwater system and a Central Tactical System.

The Falklands War – Operation Corporate

During the Falklands conflict the Nimrods received substantial modifications. For instance, with the distances involved across the South Atlantic a flight refuelling capability was paramount. BAe Woodford set to work and speedily fitted a probe to XV229 for aerodynamic tests. The probe caused aerodynamic problems and the aircraft needed a small fin under the tail and finlets on the horizontal tail maintain directional stability. The first completed conversion of a Nimrod was delivered to Kinloss and cleared for day and night refuelling on May 3.

Next the MoD demanded that Sidewinder missiles be trialled. Mountings were quickly designed for twin Sidewinders on the Nimrods unused underwing hardpoints and a trial firing took place. Harpoon missiles were also trial launched from the bomb bay. Aircraft with these refinements were designated as Nimrod MR2P. There was also an urgent need for electronic intelligence gathering and the R1s also suddenly gained flight-refuelling probes.

In May 1995 Nimrod R1 XW666 was on an air test from Kinloss when it suffered double engine fire, the wing caught fire and following two explosions the pilot opted for a crash landing in the Moray Firth. Fortunately the seven crew all escaped. As the Nimrod R1s played an invaluable role and were being updated under the Starwindow programme with new sensors, receivers, databases and workstations, the RAF decided that a MR2 ➤

Nimrod MR2P XV248 banking with its cavernous bomb bay open. During the Falklands conflict, Nimrods were equipped for flight refuelling and owing to the aerodynamic effects of the probe had fins fitted to their horizontal tailplane. *(Avro Heritage)*

Nimrod MR2P with underwing Boz pod. Note the coaster aground on the rocks. *(Avro Heritage)*

should be converted to replace it. XV249 was flown to Woodford for structural conversion to a R1 which was completed in December 1996 when it was delivered to RAF Waddington for equipment fit.

From the Falklands to Afghanistan

After 'Operation Corporate', BAe Woodford continued with Nimrod work and the final MR2, XZ284, was delivered to Kinloss in December 1985. Where Nimrods had always been tasked in the maritime role for which they had been designed, with the end of the Cold War the role of MR2 was extended to encompass land-based intelligence to ground forces.

⌄ **Dynamic view of one of the three Nimrod R1s fitted out for electronic surveillance. These aircraft had a plethora of aerials, fewer windows and no MAD boom at the tail.** *(BAE SYSTEMS North West Heritage)*

In the First Gulf War in 1990-91 five MR2s were deployed to Seeb in Oman to record all movements in the sea lanes and assist coalition warships in their attacks on enemy shipping. Only eight years later the Nimrods were back in a role supporting NATO forces in Serbia. For the Second Gulf War in 2003 six Nimrod MR2Ps received upgrades including a forward looking infra-red turret under the left wing to better support land forces and the capability to carry Boz pods with a towed radar decoy under each wing.

In Afghanistan (Operation Herrick), the Nimrods were heavily involved in land operations to identify enemy forces until their withdrawal from use. In September

2006 XV230 caught fire after refuelling in flight over Kandahar, broke up and crashed, killing 14 people. A Board of Enquiry and an Independent Review concluded that the aircraft was vulnerable to catching fire during or after in-flight refuelling and change of procedure was immediately introduced. But only 14 months later, following flight refuelling, the crew of XV235 were alerted to a serious leak and it appeared that they were saved by the procedural change. In-flight refuelling of the Nimrod was then suspended.

The 31 March 2010 saw the earlier than planned withdrawal from service of the Nimrod MR2. It had been intended that they would remain in use until the MRA4s arrived. Nimrod R1 operations ceased only 15 months later in June 2011. The withdrawal from service of the MR2 and R1s left a capability gap in signals intelligence, maritime reconnaissance, search and rescue roles.

Nimrod AEW 3

Following the issue of an Operational Requirement in 1975 for an AEW aircraft to replace the aged Shackleton AEW2, Marconi and Hawker Siddeley offered the Nimrod. A version with rotating scanner mounted above the fuselage was examined, but the project was finalised using two scanners, one mounted in the extreme nose and one in the tail, each sweeping 180° which was synchronized to provide 360° coverage. The forward radome was shaped and positioned by the constraints of aerial size, aerodynamics, pilot visibility and by ground clearance. The rear radome was mounted high on the tail to give sufficient clearance at

take-off. It had been hoped to use the same profile fore and aft, but the pointed shape of the forward radome had evolved to meet aerodynamic, bird strike and rain-erosion constraints and led to unsteady flow breakaway over a similarly shaped aft radome. As a result, a separate, more rounded profile was developed. Mounting the existing fin above the contours of the new rear fuselage improved the directional stability of Nimrod AEW in contrast to the other marks. As the bomb bay was not needed, its space was used for additional fuel tanks which could operate as heat exchangers for all the electronic equipment. The additional fuel carried naturally improved the aircraft's range.

A former BOAC Comet 4 originally bought by the MoD for radio trials work in mid-1972 registered XW826, was delivered to Woodford as development aircraft. It flew in June 1977 but was only partly representative of the projected aircraft as it only had the forward radar antenna installed.

British Aerospace's role was confined to providing the airframe, Marconi-Elliott Avionics' was to supply the radar and AEW systems which were designed from the outset to work over land and water. It had automatic initiation and tracking of targets down to small boats. The data system could be linked to ships, fighters, ground stations, tankers or other AEW aircraft. But neither contractor was in total control of the project. The Royal Air Force requirement was for eleven aircraft but no

▲ **XW626 was a former BOAC Comet 4 that was converted to carry the nose radome of the Nimrod AEW3. It made its first flight in this configuration in June 1977.**
(BAE SYSTEMS)

▼ **Nimrod AEW3 XV263.**
(BAE SYSTEMS)

new airframes were built. Instead they came from the aircraft withdrawn from Malta by 1979 and from the eight extra aircraft ordered for employment reasons in 1973 and which had been in limbo at Woodford for many months. The conversion work involved an entirely new aft fuselage and a repositioned, heightened tail.

The first of three development AEW3s, XZ286 flew on 16 July 1980 and following the other two development aircraft, first production aircraft XZ285 flew in December 1981 but it did not have a fully

functioning radar system. Four more AEW3s were completed but by then the whole project was running late and costs were rising steeply.

Nimrod AEW3 Cancelled
The project was cancelled on 18 December 1986. The RAF stated the radar and AEW systems were not functioning adequately and it was unclear as to when they would work. However it was a very complex programme and the fact it was running late was unsurprising. There are some who argue that had the ➤

programme continued, these problems would have been ironed out. The Nimrod AEW3s were cannibalised for spares, stored and then scrapped. After a considerable expense on the AEW3s the RAF was now forced to purchase the Boeing E3A AWACS. There was a five year wait for delivery from the USA, so the Shackletons AEW2s remained in use until July 1991.

Nimrod MRA4

In 1993 the MoD issued a requirement for a Maritime Patrol Aircraft to replace Nimrod MR2. At that time the RAF had 24 Nimrods in service, plus two reserves and the expectation was that 25 new aircraft would be ordered to replace these. Surprisingly the RAF's three Nimrod R1s were not included in this replacement programme.

⌃ The maiden flight of Nimrod MRA4 PA1 ZJ516 on 26 August 2004 from Woodford to Warton. Photo taken from BAE-owned Pilatus PC-9 ZG969.
(BAE SYSTEMS North West Heritage)

⌄ ZJ516 off the starboard wing of the third MRA4 ZJ517 in November 2006. The left side fuselage blister contained a Ram-Air Turbine.
(BAE SYSTEMS North West Heritage)

BAE's bid for the contract was based on a refurbished Nimrod MR2 branded as Nimrod 2000. The MoD believed using extensively refurbished aircraft was the cheaper option, although BAE would probably have preferred to design a completely new aircraft. Just like BAE all the other bidders were offering revamps of existing aircraft; Lockheed Martin had its Orion2000, Lockheed Tactical Systems UK another Orion rebuild while Breguet proposed a version of the Atlantic. Unsurprisingly BAE won the £2.4bn contract to supply 21 new aircraft in December 1996. The RAF declared that the aircraft would be known as the Nimrod Maritime Reconnaissance and Attack (MRA) Mark 4.

BAE's plan was to employ refurbished Nimrod MR2 fuselages mated to a new centre section, a new larger wing,

undercarriage, pressure floor and entirely new systems. The new wing, with 12ft more span and comprising a 23% greater area than the old MR2 wing, had four underwing hardpoints to allow the carriage of a variety of weapons including Harpoon, ASRAAM, Maverick, Sidewinder and Storm Shadow, giving the aircraft an impressive offensive capability.

The MRA4 was re-engined with four 15,500lb-thrust BMW Rolls-Royce BR710 turbofans which consumed 30% less fuel than the MR2's Speys and produced 25% more thrust, but the BR710's diameter was almost 50% greater and introduced large structural changes to the inboard wing to accommodate the four new engines. The fuselage remained almost unchanged, except for a ram-air turbine in a teardrop fairing

In 2006 the second Nimrod MRA4 prototype ZJ518 underwent extreme indoor heat trials at the McKinley Climatic Laboratory at Eglin AFB, operating in temperatures up to 44°C. *(BAE SYSTEMS North West Heritage)*

▲ **Nimrod MRA4 PA2 ZJ518.**

(BAE SYSTEMS North West Heritage)

ahead of the port wing leading edge.

It was equipped with a Boeing Tactical Command System. Sensors included the Thales Searchwater radar and for advanced visual search the Northrop Grumman Electro-optical Search and Detection System was installed in a retractable ball turret behind the nosewheel. Possibly the most significant equipment was the Israeli Electronic Support Measures Suite which provided a major Electronic

Intelligence capability. The new aircraft was also fitted with a multi-function Defensive Aids Sub-System which has Chaff and Towed Radar Decoys amongst its armoury.

Flightdeck crew was reduced from four to two, as the new Airbus-type EFIS flight management system did not require either a flight engineer or navigator. There were eight mission crew; two tactical co-coordinators, two acoustics operators, an Information

Manager and two dry operators; one for radar, one for electronic support measures and a crew member for additional tasks. The MRA4 had three fewer crew compared to the MR2.

Delays and budget overruns

The programme soon ran into problems and in October 1999 BAE brought the rebuilding of the fuselages back in-house from their subcontractors, Cobham at Bournemouth and transported them to Woodford. This put the programme 23 months back, pushing the in-service date from 2003 until at least 2005. BAE was forced to pay the government £46m in compensation. Delays continued and in 1999 the RAF had already cut its Nimrod MRA4 order from 21 to 18, citing the reduced submarine threat and the aircraft's improved capability.

Though earlier marks of the Nimrod had never achieved any export sales despite stringent efforts, BAE sought to offer the Nimrod MRA4 to the United States Navy for their Multi-mission Maritime Aircraft programme and had examined the manufacture of new Nimrod fuselages for a possible USN order. Initially BAE was teamed up with McDonnell Douglas but this ended with its takeover by Boeing. Other firms approached were convinced that either Lockheed or Boeing would win the contract – and Boeing did. As a result in 2002 BAE withdrew from the programme ➤

after failing to secure a US partner as without one there was no likelihood of their bid being accepted.

In 2003 the MoD and BAE agreed to a new contract to produce three Nimrod MRA4s to test the aircraft's aerodynamics and systems. PA01 (ZJ516) was not fitted with the Mission system but with flight test equipment. PA02 (ZJ518) was tasked with hot/cold temperature and armament trials in addition to some Mission system testing. The final test aircraft PA03 (ZJ517) was the first to be fitted with the complete Mission system.

First flight and flight testing
The first Nimrod MRA4 ZJ516 made its maiden flight from Warton and Woodford on 26 August 2004. Flight Testing was centred at Warton which monitored flights via telemetry but all updates to the test aircraft took place at Woodford which had the advantage of sufficient hangar space. The second test

Nimrod, PA02 flew in December 2004 and the third in August 2005. The Nimrod MRA4 had several handling issues; an imbalance between the elevators and ailerons, a lack of stability, a lack of a nose drop in some stalling configurations for which a stick pusher had to be introduced.

The MoD indicated that they were confident about the project and in July 2006 signed a production contract for twelve aircraft and 30 years of BAE support (which would allow the company to recoup the losses it had incurred). In May 2009 the number of aircraft to be delivered was reduced again, this time to just nine. These would be from the fourth aircraft onwards; the three development Nimrods were to be scrapped. There was some talk of these three Nimrod prototypes being configured as Nimrod R5s to replace the R1s but nothing came of it. The fourth MRA4 and the first production aircraft ZJ514 flew in September 2009, was

officially accepted by the RAF on 10 March 2010 and declared 'ready to train'. The fifth aircraft ZJ515 flew on 8 March. Everything now appeared set for the MRA4 to enter service.

Another Nimrod Cancellation
The new Coalition Government came into power in the UK in May 2010 and introduced swingeing expenditure cuts. No departments were spared and the Ministry of Defence was far over budget. Cuts were introduced in all the three services; the RAF lost its Harriers, some of its Tornados and the Nimrod MRA4 was also axed.

There was heavy criticism of the decision to scrap an aircraft with a superb capability just about to enter service and for which there was no apparent replacement. In support of the Government's decision was a large amount of ill-informed comment on the MRA4, which was tainted by its association with the terrible accident to

XV230 and rumours that the new version was also vulnerable to the same problem, but if that were the case why had the MoD accepted it? Ten of the eleven aircraft were scrapped at Woodford in January – February 2011 and ZJ514 at Warton in mid-February. The Woodford factory with its very long and great history of producing aircraft then closed for ever.

The cost to the British tax payer for 18 years' work resulting in nothing at all was circa £4bn. The Nimrod MRA4 fared no better than the AEW3 in its eventual outcome and in July 2016 the Government has now purchased nine Boeing P-8 Poseidons with the first deliveries in 2019.

Conclusions

The Nimrod MR1, R1 and MR2 were delivered by HSA/BAe to the RAF on budget and on schedule, but the later marks of the Nimrod failed to enter service. The AEW3 was apparently let down by the Marconi radar systems. The MRA4 was the victim of a Government determined to make major cuts in defence expenditure. The MRA4 could have been a superb multi-role aircraft. It had maritime and overland Combat-ISTAR (intelligence, surveillance target acquisition and reconnaissance) capability and possessed a large offensive capability married to a huge range. There were many mistakes in its implementation but it was cancelled when most of the money had already been spent. ∎

Data	Nimrod MRA4
Length	126ft 9in
Wingspan	127ft
Height	31ft
MTOW	232,315lbs
Cruising speed	570mph
Range	6910mls
Crew	10
Powerplant	4 x Rolls-Royce BR710 15,500lbs thrust
Armament	**Missiles:** Sidewinder, Martel, Harpoon, Maverick, Storm Shadow **Torpedoes:** Stingray Depth charges, Mines, Sonobuoys

The huge bomb bay of Nimrod ZJ518 open during Stingray torpedo dropping trials. Ahead of the bomb bay the Electrical-optical scanner turret can be seen in its retracted position. Behind the bomb bay the six chutes for dropping Sono-buoys can be seen.
(BAE SYSTEMS North West Heritage)

BAE SYSTEMS NIMROD MRA.4 • CUTAWAY DRAWING KEY

1. Flight refuelling probe
2. Stand-by pitot head
3. Taxying light
4. Search radar scanner
5. Nose compartment radome
6. Scanner mounting
7. ILS antenna
8. Front pressure bulkhead
9. Forward ESM antenna fairings, port and starboard
10. MLS antenna
11. Windscreen wipers
12. Electrically heated windscreen panels
13. Instrument panel shroud
14. Overhead switch panel
15. Eyebrow window
16. Pilot's seat, two-pilot flight deck
17. Direct vision window panel
18. Instrument panel with multi-function EFIS displays
19. Control column yoke
20. Side console panel with nosewheel steering tiller
21. Pitot head
22. Avionics cooling ram air intake
23. Nose undercarriage leg housing
24. Twin nosewheels, aft retracting
25. Fixed mudguards
26. Forward fuselage electrics and avionics racks
27. Cockpit roof hatch, inoperative with refuelling boom fitted
28. Starboard side forward entry door
29. TCAS antenna
30. Starboard side avionics racks
31. Crew toilet compartment
32. Ventral equipment bay
33. Nose undercarriage wheel bay
34. Electro-optical scanner turret
35. Forward weapons bay doors
36. Weapons bay 'pannier' sidewall structure
37. Port beam lookout station
38. Bulged observation window
39. Radar workstation
40. ESM workstation
41. Combined VHF/UHF/IFF antenna
42. Communications workstation
43. MLS antenna

44. TACCO 1 workstation
45. TACCO 2 workstation
46. Fully adjustable individual crew seats on sliding rail mounts
47. Emergency ram-air turbine (RAT), extended
48. RAT housing, external to fuselage pressure shell
49. Underfloor fuel cells, fore and aft
50. Acoustic operators seats (2)
51. Starboard outer engine air intake
52. GPS 1 antenna
53. MW sensor
54. Acoustic workstation
55. Underfloor hydraulics equipment bay
56. Front spar mounting fuselage main bulkhead
57. Electrical equipment racks, port and starboard
58. VHF/UHF antenna
59. Strobe light
60. Forward cabin conditioned air ducting
61. Escape hatches, port and starboard
62. Wing centre-section with integral fuel tank
63. Fuselage centre avionics equipment racks
64. GPS 2 antenna
65. Starboard outer engine bay
66. Starboard main undercarriage, stowed position
67. Semi-span stub main spar
68. Leading edge landing lights
69. Starboard underwing missile carriage
70. Leading edge de-icing air ducting
71. Starboard wing integral fuel tankage
72. Fuel transfer and vent piping
73. Fixed external fuel tank
74. Vent surge tank
75. Wing tip ESM equipment pod
76. Winglet mounted ESM antenna

77. Starboard aileron
78. Aileron tandem hydraulic actuators
79. Outboard plain flap segment, down position
80. Starboard airbrake panel (open), upper and lower surfaces
81. Fuel collector tank with boost pumps
82. Starboard hydraulic flap actuator
83. Flap interconnecting link
84. Fuel vent
85. Inboard flap segment, down position
86. Starboard engine exhaust fairing
87. ADF antenna

88. Galley
89. Dinette
90. Rear spar mounting fuselage main frame
91. Passenger seats (2)
92. Rear cabin conditioned air distribution duct
93. JTIDS antenna
94. Auxiliary power unit (APU) mounted in starboard wing root fairing
95. Sonobuoy racks, port and starboard
96. Rotary sonobuoy launchers (4)
97. Pressurised single sonobuoy launchers (2)
98. VHF/UHF antenna
99. Crew wardrobe
100. TACAN antenna

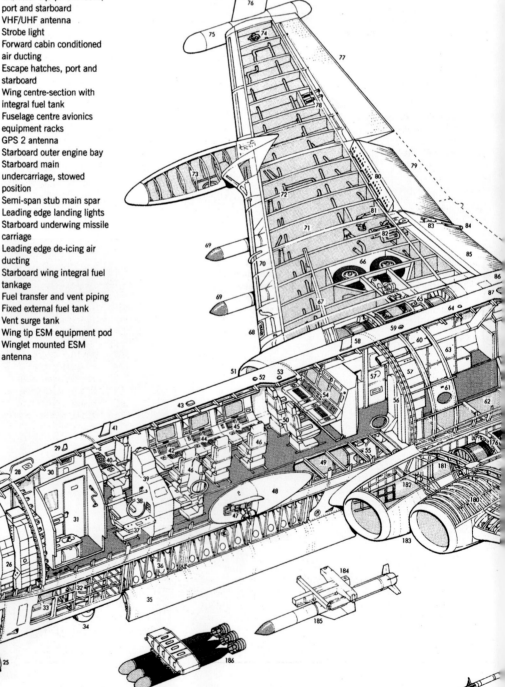

101 Conditioned air mixing ducts
102 Conditioning system ram air intake
103 Extended fin root fairing
104 Flush HF antennae
105 Fin de-icing air duct
106 Fin rib structure
107 Starboard tailplane
108 Auxiliary fins, above and below
109 Starboard elevator
110 Fin tip 'canoe' antenna fairing
111 SATCOM antenna
112 Rudder mass balance
113 Rudder rib structure
114 Tail navigation light
115 Boom housing CAE Electronics AN/ASQ-504(V) AIMS Magnetic Anomaly Detector
116 Aft ESM antennae
117 Elevator trim tab
118 Port auxiliary fins
119 Port elevator
120 Static dischargers
121 Elevator mass balance
122 Tailplane rib structure
123 Tailplane thermal leading edge de-icing
124 Fin and tailplane mounting bulkhead
125 Ventral fin
126 Tail bumper
127 HF antenna rail
128 Dual air conditioning packs
129 Fuselage rear pressure bulkhead

130 Rear fuselage avionics equipment racks, port and starboard
131 Tie-down rails, crew baggage stowage
132 Inward opening rear entry door
133 Airstairs, stowed position
134 Wing root trailing edge fairing
135 Exhaust shroud
136 Wing root fuel tank bays
137 Rear spar exhaust duct forged and machined bulkhead
138 Jet pipes
139 Port engine exhausts
140 Port inboard plain flap segment
141 Flap rib structure
142 Flap hydraulic actuator
143 Port airbrake panel, upper and lower surfaces

144 Outer plain flap segment
145 Rear spar
146 Aileron dual hydraulic actuators
147 Port aileron rib structure
148 Port winglet mounted ESM antenna
149 Port navigation light
150 Wingtip ESM pod
151 High and low band ESM antennae, fore and aft
152 Leading edge thermal de-icing ducting
153 Outer wing panel rib structure

161 AIM-9L Sidewinder self - protection air-to-air missile, potential for future integration on lateral stub pylons
162 Port wing stores pylons
163 Inboard leading edge de-icing air duct
164 Front spar
165 Port wing integral fuel tank
166 Machined wing ribs
167 Outer wing panel joint rib
168 Port main undercarriage four-wheel bogie
169 Mainwheels with multi-plate carbon brakes
170 Wheel bay with pre-closing mainwheel door
171 Breaker strut and retraction linkage
172 Hydraulic retraction jack
173 Mainwheel leg pivot mounting
174 Engine bay firewalls
175 Full authority digital engine control unit
176 Main engine mounting beams

154 Wing bottom skin/stringer panel with access manholes
155 External fuel tank mounting
156 Tank protective bumper
157 Port external fuel tank
158 Slotted tank fairing
159 AGM-84 Harpoon air-to surface anti-shipping missile
160 ALARM anti-radiation missile, capacity for future integration

177 BMW Rolls-Royce BR710 turbofan engine
178 Port semi-span main spar
179 Port landing lights
180 Intake duct frame structure
181 Forged and machined intake duct bulkhead
182 Main spar-to-centre section joint
183 Port engine air intakes
184 Weapons bay missile carrier/launcher
185 AGM-84 Harpoon, two in internal weapons bays
186 Stingray torpedoes

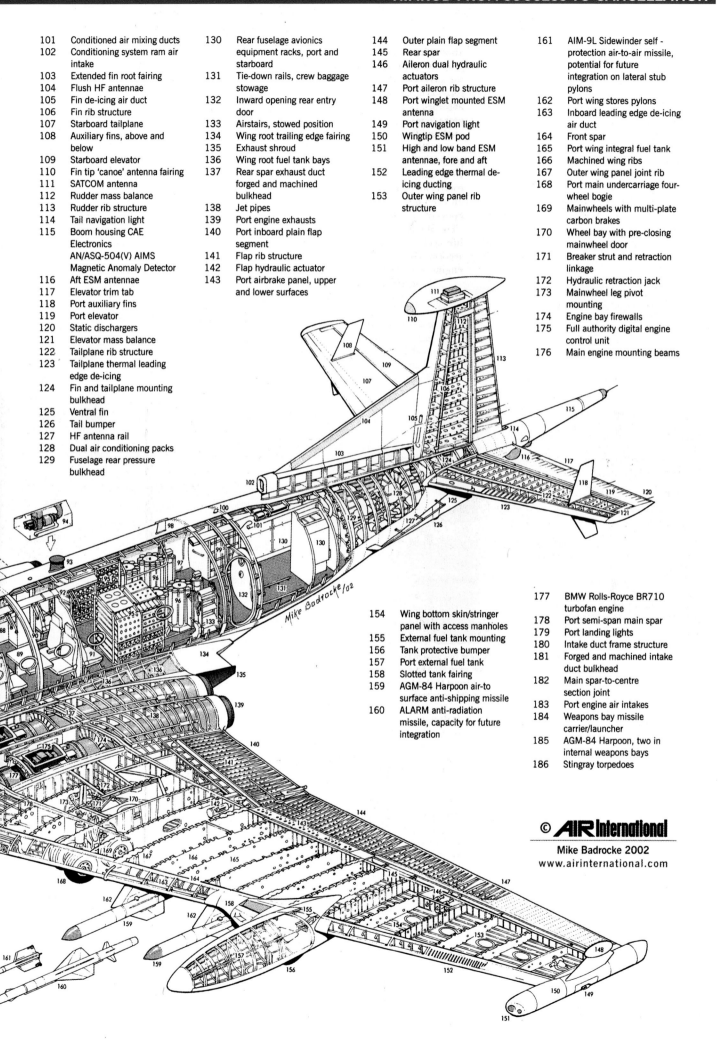

Mike Badrocke/02

© AIR International

Mike Badrocke 2002
www.airinternational.com

Jaguar - Anglo-French strike trainer

▲ The first French Jaguar single-seat prototype A03. The previous two French prototypes were twin-seaters. Note the original short fin. *(BAE SYSTEMS)*

In May 1965, the British and French Governments agreed to develop an advanced trainer/strike aircraft based on the Breguet 121 design with Bregeut taking design leadership on the airframe. Both countries initially agreed to receive 150 aircraft each with a 50/50 workshare. Breguet building the front and centre fuselage and BAC manufacturing the remainder of it. Final assembly and flight testing took place in both countries. UK final assembly and flight test was at Warton, and following Breguet's takeover by Dassault its activities were centred at Toulouse.

A joint Anglo-French firm called SEPECAT (Societé Européene de Production de l'Avion Ecole de Combat et d'Appui Tactique was set up to develop, design, co-ordinate manufacture, finance and sell the new aircraft. In February 1965 Rolls-Royce and Turbomeca had already agreed to collaborate on their respective submissions for the aircraft with the RB172T/T260 Adour. Less than a month after the agreement, and with the British car manufacturer's blessing the new aircraft was named 'Jaguar'.

The aircraft
The requirement called for Mach 1.7 at high altitude and Mach 1.1 at low altitude,

XW560, the first British prototype S06 landing at Warton. It also has the original short fin. *(BAE SYSTEMS North West Heritage)*

short take off from rough surfaces with a tactical weapons load, long range capability using internal fuel only and twin engines.

Control was by wing spoilers to provide roll control, an all-flying tailplane, air brakes and rudder. To provide short field performance in and out of rough runways the wing had leading edge slats and full-span double-slotted wing flaps.

The British and French versions

The differences between the two air forces aircraft were confined to the cockpit arrangement, ejector seats, fixed guns, refuelling probe, navigation and attack system. Each adopted very different nav/attack systems using widely different philosophies. The RAF regarded their twin-seat trainers as aircraft that could fly alongside the single-seaters during a hostile situation unlike the French which did not equip their Jaguar E for such a role.

The French and English versions

The Jaguar was initially developed into five versions for the two countries, as follows:

Armée de l'Air

Jaguar A – single-seater strike aircraft with twin DEFA 30mm cannon, five external stores points, provision for flight refuelling and nav/attack system.

Jaguar E - advanced trainer with twin DEFA 30mm cannon, five external stores points, no provision for flight refuelling. Basic nav/attack system

The final Jaguar prototype, the British B08, XW566 taking off from Warton with underwing tanks and bombs during trials. This aircraft has the taller fin. *(BAE SYSTEMS North West Heritage)*

▼ A Jaguar broken down into its component pieces in an assembly hangar at Warton. *(BAE SYSTEMS North West Heritage)*

Aeronavale

The Jaguar M (Marine) differed from all the other versions in having a strengthened airframe and undercarriage. It had single mainwheels and a twin nosewheels on an extendable nose leg for aircraft carrier catapult launching, and was designed for the higher descent rates needed for deck landing. The Jaguar M, like all the other versions, was equipped with an arrester hook, though stressed for higher loads. Production Jaguar M would have had twin DEFA 30mm cannon, flight-refuelling and a nav/attack system similar to the Jaguar E.

The Jaguar M flew in prototype form but was not otherwise proceeded with. The other variants received much additional and different equipment with the passage of time.

RAF

Jaguar S – single seater strike aircraft with twin Aden 30mm cannon, five external stores points, provision for flight refuelling

and sophisticated nav/attack system.

Jaguar B – twin-seater trainer with one DEFA 30mm cannon, five external stores points, no provision for flight refuelling and sophisticated nav/attack system as Jaguar S.

The Jaguar prototypes

It was decided to build eight prototypes. Four for the Armée de l'Air flew first, E01 and E02 twin-seaters and the two single seaters, A03 and A04 which flew in numerical order. M05 was the prototype for the Aeronavale and then came three British built prototypes, two single-seaters, S06 and S07 and finally B08 a twin-seater. Each of them was allotted specific roles in the test programme.

The first flight of E01 finally took place on 8 September 1968 with Breguet's Chief Test Pilot, Bernard Witt at the controls at Istres. The other prototypes followed in early 1969. The first British prototype S06

registered XW560 first flew piloted by Jimmy Dell on 12 October 1969 and S07, XW563 flew on 12 June 1970. The final and eighth prototype, B08 XW566 built to production standard flew on 30 August 30 1971 with Paul Millet at the controls.

During the test programme, various external refinements were made to the design including revised nosewheel doors, engine air intakes and spine contours (to house an improved air-conditioning system), cambered tailplane and a fin of increased area. The ventral fins were added early in the test programme to improve stability while the airbrakes were enlarged and perforated during development flying.

Engine problems

During the early years of flight testing problems with the Adour caused frequent hold-ups to flying, and a very high engine failure rate. From September 1971 prototype E02 was based at Warton for

three years, during which it was used by Rolls-Royce/Turbomeca for Adour development. The Adour powerplant was still a poor and erratic performer even after two years and 1,000 flying hours.

Test flying losses

During the test programme, aside from the ongoing issues with the Adour engines, very few serious development problems arose, although some delay resulted from the loss of three of the five prototypes. The first aircraft E01 crashed on approach to Istres in March 1970 when it appeared that an engine had failed and the pilot shut down the other engine in error. A03 was written off after a heavy landing in February 1972 and S06 XW560 after an engine fire during ground running at the A&AEE Boscombe Down in August 1972. By the end of 1973, with production aircraft entering service, the development programme was declining in intensity and trials shifted on to more esoteric items, such as spinning which required a considerable amount of analysis and dangerous test-flying and subsequent modification.

Production

The final number of Jaguars received by the two air arms was 400. Britain dropped the Jaguar from the training role reducing its order to 35 trainers while increasing its single-seater order to 165. France also modified its order and received 160 Jaguar A strike aircraft and only 40 Jaguar E trainers.

In service with the French Air Force

The French Jaguars entered service in 1973 were gradually formed into nine squadrons (three of which were nuclear strike) plus a tactical navigation unit. Unlike British Jaguars they never received upgraded Adour engines so take off performance from airfields in high temperatures zones often proved poor. Nor did the French Jaguars receive the overwing missile pylons retrofitted to the RAF fleet but they did get nav/attack modifications and other major additions to their weaponry.

French Jaguars were employed against insurgents in Senegal and Mauretania in 1977, in Chad the following year and until 1987 against a Libyan-backed insurgency. In 1991, 28 French Jaguars were sent to the Gulf as part of 'Operation Desert Storm' to counter the Iraqi invasion of Kuwait. Cuts were made to the size of the Jaguar force after the Gulf operation but they were still an asset for the French forces. They flew bombing missions over Bosnia in 1993 and Kosovo in 1999. After 32 years operational history they were withdrawn from service in July 2005

In service with the RAF

The RAF's Jaguars appeared distinctively different appearance from their French counterparts with their chisel nose window for the laser rangefinder and marked target seeker (LRMTs), which was an aid to automatic weapon release.

First deliveries of the Jaguar began at Lossiemouth at the end of May 1973 and others gradually followed with training courses beginning there in February 1974. At its peak the Jaguar equipped eight units

▲ **XX733 Jaguar GR1 of RAF No 6 Squadron.** *(BAE SYSTEMS North West Heritage)*

in Britain and Germany, playing an important NATO strike and reconnaissance role. Paradoxically it was only after the end of the Cold War that the Jaguar was used in a conflict when it was employed in 1991 as part to drive Iraqi forces out of Kuwait.

Prior to 'Operation Desert Storm', the Jaguars received improvements to the engine, better chaff dispensers and overwing missile pylons as fitted to the

Jaguar International. Jaguars continued over Iraq after the cessation of hostilities as part of 'Operation Northern Watch' to contain Iraqi activities against the Kurds. Jaguars flew similar operations over the former Yugoslavia in 1996. After these operations the aircraft received an avionics upgrade including Thermal Imaging Airborne Laser Designation (TIALD) pod for self-designation of targets and the

Jaguar GR3 XZ109 of No 6 Sqn taxiing with flight refuelling probe extended and overwing pylons. The Jaguar export version, the Jaguar International, introduced overwing missile racks and these were retrofitted to RAF Jaguars. *(BAE SYSTEMS North West Heritage)*

uprated and more economical Adour 106 engines. With these modifications, the GR1 became a GR3A and the T2 a T4.

The Jaguar was withdrawn from RAF service as a cost-saving measure, two years earlier than planned in 2007.

Jaguar International

Dassault took over Breguet in 1971 and then the relationship with BAC became difficult, as Dassault regarded their 50% share in Jaguar unfavourably in contrast to their own Mirage F1, which they wholly produced. This manifested itself in

▼ FAE302, one of twelve Ecuadorian Jaguars, on approach to land. They were operated from 1977 until 2004. *(BAE SYSTEMS North West Heritage)*

Dassault competing against Jaguar with its Mirage for many overseas contracts, which on some occasions had the opposite effect of allowing American aircraft to win the order. In 1980 British Aerospace obtained full rights from Dassault to export Jaguar, but often this was then in direct opposition to the Mirage F1.

The Jaguar International based on the RAF version was announced at the 1974 Farnborough Air Show. The first production RAF Jaguar S1, XX108, which was retained for trials, was presented statically at the Show as the prototype of this version with a huge variety of weapons on display, including an Agave radar nose as later fitted to the Indian Air Forces Jaguar IM variant. Trials of the actual Jaguar International specification on XX108 began the following year with Adour 804s installed, providing a

much-improved performance with Magic missiles on over-wing mountings which allowed the full range of weapons to be carried on the under-wing positions.

Export orders

Ecuador and Oman each ordered ten Jaguar single-seaters and two trainers for delivery in 1977-78. Oman re-ordered the same number in 1980 which were all delivered by the end of 1983. The first production Jaguar International, a twin-seater for Ecuador FAE283 temporarily registered as G27-266 flew in August 1976. After steady usage by 1991 the Ecuadorian Air Force only had nine Jaguars flying and so topped up its fleet with three attrition replacements GR1s from RAF which were refurbished by BAe at Warton. However in 2004 Ecuador withdrew its aircraft from service. In a similar fashion, Oman added to its Jaguar

Two Jaguars leaving on delivery to Oman, which operated 24 aircraft from 1977 until 2014. *(BAE SYSTEMS North West Heritage)*

JS126 – JS134, nine of the 35 Indian Air Force Jaguars single-seaters assembled at Warton as part of the large Indian order for 130 Jaguars. There were also three twin-seaters assembled at Warton, 45 completed from SEPECAT kits in Bangalore and further aircraft were mainly built from Indian parts in India. *(BAE SYSTEMS North West Heritage)*

fleet with a former RAF T2 and a GR1 and contracted BAe Warton to carry out a nav/attack upgrade on all its remaining fleet between 1986 and 1989. The Omani Jaguars were retired in 2014.

After lengthy negotiations Nigeria became the final customer for the Jaguar International with an order for 18, all built to the final Jaguar International standard with Adour 811 engines. These Jaguars were the final ones manufactured. The Nigerian aircraft had a short life serving from 1984 until 1991 when they were withdrawn from use.

▼Nigeria received 18 Jaguars from 1984 but they were retired only seven years later. NAF 705 bearing 'B' markings G27-392.
(BAE SYSTEMS North West Heritage)

Indian Air Force order

In the 1970s India was seeking to become self-reliant and would only consider those aircraft where licence production in India was possible. After considering the Mirage F1 and Saab Viggen, in October 1978 the Indian Government chose the Jaguar because it fulfilled the IAF's requirements, was the most economical, could be delivered ahead of its two competitors and was the only twin-engined aircraft in the field.

Negotiations were completed with BAe in April 1979 for a total of 168 aircraft

to be built. Warton was to build 38, then 45 assembled by Hindustan Aircraft Ltd (HAL) at Bangalore from kits provided by SEPECAT, and then an increasing proportion of Indian components would be employed and from 1984 the Jaguars would be entirely Indian built. For the Indian Air Force's immediate needs the RAF loaned 18 Jaguars, including two trainers trained pilots and ground crew. The IAF eventually received twenty Jaguar IB (India B) twin-seaters, 136 Jaguar IS (India Strike) single-seaters and twelve Jaguar IM (India Maritime) single-seat

Data	Jaguar International
Length	55ft 2½in
Wingspan	28ft 6in
Height	16ft ½in
MTOW	34,612 lb
Max speed	M1.6 (high altitude) M1.1 (low altitude)
Range	875mls (combat)
Crew	1/2
Powerplant:	Rolls-Royce/Turbomeca 811 8,400 lb with reheat
Armament	2 x 30mm cannon, Missiles: Sidewinder, Martel Sea Eagle, Bombs etc

They are used in ground and maritime attack roles, and the upgraded types are set to receive MBDA's ASRAAM short-range air-to-air missile and Textron Defence Systems' CBU-105 Sensor Fused Weapon. Delhi has also planned to re-engine the Jaguar fleet with HAL-built Honeywell F125-IN engines, but that programme currently appears to have suffered a delay.

anti-shipping strike aircraft fitted with the Agave radar and Sea Eagle missile.

India is the sole remaining operator of the Jaguar, with approximately 120 in service which are shortly to receive the Darin 3 upgraded avionics package. The design and development of this new avionics suite was carried out by HAL's mission and combat system research and design centre, with the overhaul completed at its Bengaluru facility. Five IAF squadrons are equipped with Jaguars.

⌄ Indian Air Force J1001 and J1008 in flight. The Indian Air Force Jaguars are still regarded as a potent part of the country's arsenal. *(BAE SYSTEMS North West Heritage)*

Conclusion

British and French operations with the Jaguar operations may have ceased but 48 years after its maiden flight, the utility and longevity of the design is self-evident as it plays an important role with the Indian Air force and will do so for quite some time to come. ∎

The Multi-Role Tornado

The first prototype Tornado D-9591 bearing Panavia livery taking off on its maiden flight from Manching piloted by BAC's Chief Test Pilot, Paul Millett on 14 August 1974. The MBB Chief Test Pilot Neils Meister occupied the rear seat, but piloted the second flight. *(BAE SYSTEMS)*

The first multi-national Tornado took to the air on 14 August 1974, so when BAe came into being in 1977 the test programme was well underway, as ten prototypes had already flown. Prior to receiving its name, the Tornado had been known as the MRCA (Multi-Role Combat Aircraft) and it was a joint British, German and Italian project for which a managing company called

▼ XX946, the first British-assembled Tornado and second aircraft to fly, flying with its wings swept forward.
(BAE Systems)

Panavia was formed. The British partner company was the British Aircraft Corporation.

The Tornado's gestation was very lengthy. Following the cancellation of the BAC TSR2 in April 1965 it appeared that the RAF was to have a mixed fleet of American-built F-111Ks and the smaller Anglo-French variable-geometry (AFVG) aircraft, built by BAC in collaboration with Dassault. The AFVG with a top speed of

Mach 2+ was to replace the RAF's Lightning and the French Air Force's Mirage 3 in the air defence role and the Canberras, Buccaneers and Phantoms operated by the British in the strike role. Variable-geometry allowed the wings of the aircraft to sweep forward to provide high-lift, good manouevrability and low speeds for take-off and landing. Swept back, the wings gave low drag, low gust response conferring good transonic and supersonic performance.

The UK Government's F-111K / AFVG scheme was short-lived. In mid-1967 the French withdrew from the AFVG and at the end of 1967 the Labour Government cancelled the F-111K owing to escalating costs, but funded BAC to continue work on a UKVG project until June 1969. This provided continuity of design, wind tunnel and materials testing for BAC. The ongoing work strengthened the basis for the huge UK input into MRCA (Multi-Role Combat Aircraft) which became the Tornado and which in turn led to Eurofighter Typhoon.

Joint Working Group

In July 1968 Britain was invited to join a Joint Working Group of European countries and Canada formed to find a Lockheed F-104 replacement. Britain's presence was significant as it had the greatest expertise in advanced combat aircraft design. Several countries abandoned the project, leaving Britain, Germany and Italy. Britain offered a VG

First Italian prototype X-586 (MM586), having engine runs. This aircraft, which was the fifth prototype, flew at Caselle in December 1975. It was badly damaged on landing on its fifth flight and was taken out of the flight test programme for more than two years. *(BAE Systems)*

design similar to the final one selected for MRCA while Messerschmitt-Bőlkow-Blohm (MBB) also proposed a VG design. The final compromise used most of the BAC offering; a high wing with elevons but using the wing pivot positioning favoured by MBB.

Programme launch

The MRCA programme was launched in December 1968 and in March 1969 a tripartite-owned company called Panavia was formed with its headquarters in Munich. As it was initially understood that Germany's requirement would be the largest, MBB held 50% of the shares, BAC had 33% and Fiat just 17%. Fiat's participation rested on its desire for experience of leading-edge high technology programme as the likelihood of its Government affording Tornado was slim. Both MBB and Fiat looked to BAC, as Germany and to an even greater extent, Italy, had never mounted an aircraft programme of this magnitude and their industries did not have the experience of designing and building many of the very advanced systems which were essential for the MRCA type of aircraft.

When the size of the German order diminished from 700 to 320 the shareholdings were adjusted to better represent expected production and BAC and MBB each held 42½% while Fiat had 15%. At the same time the distinct MRCA design emerged albeit in single-seater and the twin-seater versions. Britain

▲ **BAe Test Pilot Keith Hartley conducts the 'cockpit habitability trial' in his open top Tornado XZ630.**
(BAE SYSTEMS North West Heritage)

wanted the twin-seater and in March 1970 all three parties accepted it as the basis for the MRCA. Standardising on a twin-crew cockpit allowed for a navigator, or a trainee pilot operating dual flying controls in the rear cockpit. Its multi-role specification required it to carry out close air-to-ground support, air superiority, interdiction, reconnaissance and maritime strike.

The design

BAC applied its unique experience with the recent research, design, development

and limited flight test of TSR2 to the design. For instance, where MBB had initially decided on placing the tailplane higher on the rear of the fuselage, BAC's view prevailed and its preference for low-set elevons were agreed. In a similar fashion the Corporation's experience with full-span flaps, intake positioning and control systems were applied to MRCA. BAC engineers had also learnt from engine accessibility challenges on TSR2 and were insistent that the engine panels should swing down to allow the engines to be removed downwards rather than ➤

slide backwards out of the aircraft.

The MRCA was appreciably smaller than TSR2 because of the adoption of efficient VG wings and state-of-the-art engines which were light, compact and powerful and had excellent fuel consumption characteristics. It benefited from compactness but because of radar dish size the nose cone housing the radar could not be significantly scaled down and it was large in proportion to the remainder of the aircraft. An advantage to the crew who benefited from ergonomically good cockpit characteristics.

The MRCA is controlled by a triplex fly-by-wire system with a fully-powered rudder and all-flying elevons. The elevons operate in harmony for longitudinal control and differentially for roll control, augmented in the latter task by spoilers on the upper wing which operate together as lift dumpers after touchdown. In addition, large air brakes are positioned either side of the fin.

The wing has full length leading-edge slats, double-slotted flaps, spoilers and Krueger flaps under the leading edges of the fixed inboard wing. The wing is swept fully forward for take-off and landing providing the best low speed handling; mid-sweep offers best agility while fully-swept is the configuration for high speeds. The undercarriage has a single wheel main gear and a twin wheel nose assembly each of which retracts forwards into the airframe.

Go ahead

British, West German and Italian Governments agreed in May 1969 to a joint development and production programme for the MRCA. Finally, Britain

▲ Tornado P08 XX950 at the Farnborough Air Show in 1976 with an array of the weapons the Interdictor/Strike variant could carry.
(BAE Systems)

was to build a VG aircraft – or at least part of one. Even though final assembly would take place in each of the participating countries, BAC was to build all the noses and tails, Germany each centre-section and Italy the wings. English was chosen as the project language.

The Turbo-Union RB199

A tripartite engine company, Turbo-Union was formed on 1 June 1969 with its headquarters in Bristol after Rolls-Royce won this key contract to supply its new

RB199 engine for MRCA and not the competing Pratt & Whitney TF-30. The disadvantage was that the RB199 only existed on paper while the TF-30 was already in service. The Germans were favourably inclined to an American bid, so to ensure it wouldn't be outdone, Rolls-Royce made a keenly competitive offer neither Germany nor Italy could refuse. Rolls-Royce and Motoren–Turbinen-Union (MTU) each had a 40% holding in Turbo-Union and Fiat a minority 20% share.

German, British and Italian Tornados marking the 35th anniversary of the Tri-National Tornado Training Establishment *(TTTE)* at the RIAT event in 2015. *(Author)*

A 12 Squadron Tornado GR4 flying through the 'Mach Loop' in Wales. *(BAE SYSTEMS North West Heritage)*

BAC was uneasy about the challenge of flying the combination of a new airframe and a new engine and would have preferred to have been able to use an existing, tried and tested powerplant. The engine had to be created to a very short timescale. The timing proved most unfortunate, as problems developed with the RB199 engine which coincided with Rolls-Royce's entry into receivership, resulting in nationalisation in 1971.

Maiden flight

Each country flew an allotted number of prototypes and tested them from their bases; BAC at Warton, MBB at Manching and Fiat at Caselle. Nine prototypes (P.01-09) were provided for in the tripartite Memorandum of Understanding, plus one non-flying example (P.10) assembled at Warton for static testing. Six pre-production machines were also built (P.11-16).

The first flight was scheduled for December 1973 and this target appeared easy to achieve as the first prototype D-9591 (98+04) was completed at Ottobrunn in February 1973 and moved by road to Manching. The Germans had insisted on this honour as at the time they were buying the largest number of aircraft but Sir Freddie Page (BAC Military Aircraft Division Managing Director) ensured in return that a British pilot, Paul Millett, would fly it with his German counterpart Neils Meister in the back seat.

Following reassembly at Manching trials ensued to check all the systems, the engines and the telemetry. Non-flight RB199s were used for initial ground running and taxiing tests. When flight cleared, engines arrived and were installed the compressor of the left one exploded during its first full power run. Four months later, on 14 August 1974 it finally made its first flight, climbing to 10,000 ft and performing well. On the second flight the wings were swept for the first time without any problems in trim or aerodynamics. On the subsequent flight the pilots reversed positions and then the German test pilots took over the testing of the P.01. The first aircraft's initial role was to expand and confirm the flight envelope and general handling. Later in the test programme P.01 took on other roles including engine and thrust reverser development.

Gradually the Tornado prototypes take to the air

In September, the MRCA was formally named the Tornado and on 30 October 1974, P.02 registered XX946 made its maiden flight from Warton. The flight covered the flight envelope cleared by the first prototype, including a short supersonic run concluding with low level swept wing passes and a full roll over the airfield for the benefit of the watching workforce. P.02 had an eventful life, tasked with flight-refuelling trials, external stores carriage, high incidence and spinning trials. The clearance of Tornado for airborne refuelling in July 1975 allowed test flights to be prolonged with sorties of nearly two hours rather than one hour. XX947, the third Tornado prototype and first with dual controls, made a supersonic first flight on 5 August, from Warton.

The fourth Tornado P.04 registered D-9592 (98+05) flew from Manching and the fifth P.05 X-586 (MM586), the first Italian machine, flew at Caselle in December 1975. On only its fifth flight P.05 was badly damaged on landing and was taken out of the flight test programme for more than two years. Its test roles of flutter and load measurement were taken over by BAC's P.02. The sixth prototype XX948 was another British machine and was the first to incorporate a slimmer rear fuselage and the twin Mauser cannon. (Tornados carried one or two Mauser 27mm cannon, located on the lower front fuselage.) P.06 tested performance and drag, stores-handling, rapid rolling and gun-firing. The seventh, 98+06 and eighth prototypes, XX950 flew from Manching and Warton respectively and engaged in weapons trials. The final prototype P.09 X-587(MM587) flew from Caselle on the same day, in February 1977 as P.11, the first dual-control German

▲ Two RAF Tornado GR4s carrying Brimstone missiles under the fuselage, Alarm missiles on the wing pylons and underwing tanks. *(BAE SYSTEMS)*

➤ A dramatic shot of Tornado F2 ZA254 taking off at the Farnborough Air Show in 1982. *(BAE SYSTEMS North West Heritage)*

▼ Tornado GR4 ZG750, celebrating 25 years of the type on operations, landing at the Farnborough Air Show on 14 July 2016. *(Author)*

aircraft and the first of six pre-production machines. The pre-production aircraft were typically employed at military test centres undertaking trials as a prelude to squadron service. Of these the last four pre-series aircraft were later refurbished and issued to the services.

By February 1978 the unladen aircraft had achieved over Mach 1.9 at altitude, and Mach 1 plus at low level. Acceleration was impressive; it could reach 30,000ft in two minutes from a standing start. Owing to continuing engine problems it was not until March 1979 that P.02 achieved Mach 2.

Production orders

Despite criticism of Tornado in each of the producing countries, there was the general acceptance that Tornado project costs had been kept under control and no other aircraft existed that could fulfill the role. Accordingly in 1976 the first production order was placed and further batches followed until the completion of production in 1999.

The final production contracts including attrition replacements was UK 228 IDS (Interdictor/Strike) and 173 ADV (Air Defence Variant), Germany 357 IDS and Italy 99 IDS. In addition, Saudi Arabia received 96 IDS and 24 ADV Tornadoes, all of which were assembled at Warton. Of the 977 Tornadoes built, Warton assembled 527.

The Tornado in service
Trinational Tornado Training

On 1 July 1980, two Royal Air Force

Tornado GR1s flew into RAF Cottesmore, the first arrivals at the new Trinational Tornado Training Establishment (TTTE). Just as the aircraft, engines and avionics were tripartite so too was the training. Until 1999 British, German and Italian crews were based there to complete a common operational conversion course.

The RAF's IDS Tornados

As the RAF's Vulcans were having their moment of glory over the Falklands Islands in 1982, their replacement aircraft, the Tornado, was entering service with the RAF. In total eleven squadrons were formed over time, the first three were UK-based but the remainder were based in Germany, part of the front-line defence against the Warsaw Pact nations. These squadrons and could carry both conventional and nuclear weapons and their low-level attack capability was particularly important in this NATO role. Yet it was not until after the end of the Cold War that the Tornado GR1s were tested in action and in a very different theatre. As part of the RAF contingent in the 1991 Gulf War almost sixty Tornados were employed suffering significant attrition when six aircraft were lost.

The RAF Tornado GR1 proved itself not only in the Gulf War but also Kosovo, Iraq and Afghanistan as an exceedingly capable ground-attack aircraft. Between 1997 and 2003, 142 Tornado GR1 were

▲ **Tornado F3s ZG735, ZE758 and ZE291 of 229 OCU, 29 Squadron and 5 Squadron over RAF Coningsby.**
(Key Publishing)

➤ **A Tornado F3 with Skyflash and Sidewinder missiles.**
(BAE SYSTEMS North West Heritage)

upgraded to GR4 standard by BAE Systems at Warton. Since entering service in 1981 the GR1 had developed into a number of sub-fleets with varying equipment standards. One of the main objectives of the conversion was to have a common standard of equipment throughout all the aircraft, except the Tornado GR1As which kept their sideways-looking and linescan infra-red systems and became GR4As. The GR4 can be distinguished from the GR1 by the additional fairing under the nose to house the Forward Looking Infra-Red (FLIR) and

the removal of one of its two 27mm Mauser cannon. During the conversion, major new systems were installed and the GR4 and GR4A became more potent with additional and more powerful weapons.

The first Tornado GR4 returned to front-line service in May 1998 becoming fully operational until 2001. The final example was delivered from Warton in 2003. The GR4 remains a formidable ground-attack aircraft with its sophisticated weapons suite consisting of: Brimstone, Storm Shadow, Paveway 2-4, Mauser 27mm cannon and ASRAAM.

Bearing the temporary UK military serial ZH917, one of the RSAF Tornados at Warton for the Tornado Sustainment Programme which began in 2006. *(BAE SYSTEMS North West Heritage)*

Temporarily registered as ZE114, RSAF Tornado IDS landing Warton in 2016. *(BAE SYSTEMS North West Heritage)*

In 2011 RAF Tornados were yet again involved in strike operations to help protect the rebels against Government forces in Libya and they are currently on active service as part of 'Operation Shader' on strike missions against Daesh in Iraq and Syria. All the RAF's Tornados are currently due to be retired from RAF service in 2019, with a gradual run down from 2018.

The RAF's Air Defence Variant Tornado

Unlike the IDS Tornados which were designed and built to the requirements of the three partner countries, the Tornado ADV (Air Defence Variant) was developed solely for the RAF as a long-range interceptor to replace the Lightning and the Phantom in their air defence role against an incursion by Warsaw Pact forces. Initially the IDS Tornado was considered for the air defence role and it could fulfill aspects of the requirement. However, it needed provision for air-to-air missiles and an intercept radar to replace its existing attack and terrain-following radars. Despite an RAF evaluation of American types including the F-14 Tomcat, F-15 Eagle and F-16 of and the selection of the F-15 as the most suitable, the final decision by the RAF was to seek a development of the Tornado, which was good news for BAe and financially a sensible choice when considering the cost of import, training and spares commonality.

The Tornado ADV embodied aerodynamic refinements and could easily be distinguished from the IDS owing to its longer nose radome for the Marconi Foxhunter AI.24 radar and four-foot front fuselage extension which increased internal fuel capacity and reduced drag. The lengthened fuselage provided space for four semi-recessed Skyflash air-to-air missile missiles in the underside of the fuselage. The leading edge of the fixed part of the wing was extended forwards sharpening its angle to the wing, so that when the wings were fully swept back the wings had a concave interface, rather than the convex form on the IDS. The ADV had uprated RB.199s producing 17,000lb thrust. Though the ADV was destined only for the RAF, like the strike variant it was a Panavia aircraft and work was shared among all three participating countries just as with the IDS variant. However manufacture of the four foot fuselage plug and final assembly of the aircraft was carried out at Warton. Altogether 165 of the 385 RAF Tornados were Tornado ADV interceptors.

The first Tornado ADV prototype A.01 registered ZA254 flew on 27 October 1979 piloted by Warton's Chief Test Pilot, David Eagles. The maiden flight was very successful with the aircraft airborne for 92 minutes and reaching Mach 1.2. By flight three it had achieved Mach 1.75. The F2 flight test programme developed very successfully, except for the radar whose development ran far behind schedule. Two more prototypes soon followed. By the end of the year the F2 had reached the important psychological goal of Mach 2 and two years later cleared Mach 2.16. Throughout the following year an intensive test programme took place at Warton for all the three prototypes.

An improved version of the Tornado's power plant (the RB199-34R Mk 104) was produced by Rolls-Royce offering a significant increase in thrust and incorporating a fourteen-inch longer jet-pipe. In the winter of 1982/3 Tornado prototype ZA267 had the new engine and enlarged reheat system installed which entailed a slight lengthening of the rear fuselage. ZA267 flew with the new engine in April 1983 and effectively became the prototype for the F3. The first eighteen ADVs were completed as F2s with the lower-powered RB199 of which the first six F2s were dual stick trainers. All subsequent aircraft had the higher-powered Mk 104 and were designated as Tornado F3. The Tornado F3 entered service with the RAF in 1986 and deliveries were completed seven years later. The only other customer for the F3 was the Royal Saudi Air Force which ordered twenty-four.

The RAF's F2s entered service without its Foxhunter and concrete ballast in its place but with the advent of the F3 a year later in 1986 these problems had been solved. Seven squadrons were formed, later reduced to five by the 'Peace Dividend' of 1990. With the introduction into service of the Eurofighter Typhoon in 2010 the number of Tornado F3 squadrons fell to just one, No.111 Squadron at Leuchers, near Edinburgh, and in March 2011 the Tornado F3 was retired from active service.

Tornado Export

The only export customer for Tornado was the Kingdom of Saudi-Arabia which had previously been a customer and satisfied user of the BAC Warton-built Lightning. In 1984 Saudi pilots evaluated the Tornado at Honington and in September 1985 the Kingdom ordered 48 IDS and 24 ADV Tornados. This contract also included the delivery of BAe Hawks and Pilatus PC-9 trainers. To expedite deliveries to Saudi Arabia, 18 RAF and two Luftwaffe IDS Tornados were diverted to the RSAF. The Saudi Air Force also received its 24 ADV Tornados ahead of schedule when the RAF agreed to give up delivery positions to it. In 1993 there was a follow-on order for 48 more Tornado IDSs by the RSAF, bringing its total up to 120.

The RSAF Tornados were formed into two IDS and one ADV squadron. The first IDS squadron to operate the aircraft was No 7 which came up to strength with 20 aircraft in October 1987. Next came the delivery of 24 ADVs which were equivalent to the initial batch of the RAF's F3s with deliveries beginning in February 1989. Deliveries of both IDS and ADV Tornados was completed by January 1992.

Saudi Arabia employed both its IDS and ADV aircraft in the 1991 Gulf War

⌃ Italian Air Force Tornado IDS 50-05 at the RIAT Fairford 2015. *(Author)*

against Iraq following the occupation of Kuwait. They also took part in Desert Storm where they flew 451 sorties. Beginning in 2006, 70 RSAF Tornado IDS aircraft were returned to Warton as part of the RSAF Tornado Sustainment Programme (TSP) to upgrade its fleet. The objective of the TSP was to modify Saudi Tornados in a similar fashion to the work carried out on RAF GR4s. The first part of the work was carried out in the UK and part two in Saudi Arabia. In 2006 the RSAF decided to retire its ADV aircraft and these were sold back to BAE as part of the Typhoon contract, after which they were stripped for spares. The RSAF's IDS Tornados remain in service; they were in action against ISIS targets in Syria in 2014

and in Yemen in 2015 and 2016.

German Air Force and Navy

The German Air Force (Luftwaffe) and Navy (Marine) received a total of 357 IDS Tornados including four pre-production machines. Of these all but thirty-five were IDS variants. The others were Electronic Combat and Reconnaissance (ECR) variant. The ECR prototype was a converted production model IDS and first flew in August 1988 with production deliveries beginning in 1990.

The first German Tornado Squadron formed by the Navy as MFG1 became fully operational at the beginning of 1984. Eventually a second MFG was also formed. As part of the Cold War fleet

Tornado F3s from RAF. This 24-strong fleet was made up of 20 F3s plus four F3Ts twin-stick trainers.

The importance of Tornado to BAe/BAE SYSTEMS

Nearly 1,000 Panavia Tornado aircraft were produced and delivered to the air forces of Italy, Germany, the United Kingdom and Saudi-Arabia. The last aircraft was delivered to the RSAF in March 1998, making the Tornado the largest European military aircraft co-operative programme at that time.

Tornado enabled BAC/BAe to finally utilise its variable-geometry experience and to produce a fine aircraft in collaboration with others. The threat of cancellation so prevalent in British aircraft projects was diminished by the very nature of an international collaborative programme. It has proved to be a fine war machine as exemplified by the RAF's employment of it in eleven offensive operations from 'Operation Granby' in 1990 through to 'Operation Shader' in 2017. ■

Data	Tornado GR4
Length	54ft 10in
Wingspan	45ft 7½in (extended) 28ft 2½in (fully swept)
Height	18ft 8½in
MTOW	60,000 lb
Max speed	M2.2 (high altitude) M1.1 (low altitude
Range	810 mls (combat)
Crew	2
Powerplant	Turbo-Union RB199 mk 103 2 x 17,270 lb with reheat
Armament	1 x 27mm Mauser cannon, Brimstone, Storm Shadow, Paveway 2-4, ASRAAM

reductions MFG1 was disbanded in 1993 and MFG2 also stood down in 2005. Fifty-one of the Marine's Tornados then became part of the Luftwaffe as a dedicated Reconnaissance Wing and the Marine's anti-shipping strike role was passed to the Luftwaffe.

Initially when the Tornados entered service they formed five Luftwaffe strike wings. In August 1995 these Tornados had the distinction of flying the Luftwaffe's first offensive action since the end of World War Two when its ECR Tornados destroyed anti-aircraft radars with HARM missiles during the Balkan Conflict. Tornados have continued to be deployed in offensive operations and from 2007 to 2010 six aircraft operated in Afghanistan in support of the Allied Mission.

By 2010 the number of German Tornados has been reduced to just eighty-five ECR/RECCE variants as the IDS aircraft are not being upgraded and are gradually being phased out with the delivery of the Eurofighter Typhoons. The eighty-five aircraft remaining in service have received life extension and comprehensive modernisation programmes, weapons improvements plus a software update. The German Tornados planned out-of-service date is 2025.

Italian Air Force

The Aeronautica Militare Italiana received 99 newly built Tornado IDSs plus one refurbished pre-production aircraft, P.14. The first Italian Tornado registered MM50000 flew in September 1981 and deliveries to the Air Force began in May of the following year and were completed in 1986. Italian Tornados initially served in four squadrons and had nuclear capability

under ultimate US control within NATO. Following delivery, twelve were rebuilt as Electronic Combat and Reconnaissance (ECR) similar to the German versions. Italian Tornados have been employed in the 1991 Gulf War, over Bosnia, Kosovo and currently in Afghanistan.

Owing to the late delivery of Eurofighter in the early 1990s the Italian Air Force had to find a temporary and partial replacement for its ageing Lockheed F-104s. While 60 of the F-104s could be upgraded this was well below the number of air defence aircraft required so from 1995 until 2004 the Italian Air Force leased air defence variant

On 14 August 2014 Panavia celebrated the 40th anniversary of the Tornado with a flying display and party in Manching. This RAF GR4 ZD844 is properly adorned too. *(BAE SYSTEMS)*

Hawk – 40 years of refinement

XX154, the first Hawk made its maiden flight on the evening of 21 August 1974 from Dunsfold. *(BAE Systems)*

I t is unlikely that those gathered at the Hawker Siddeley airfield at Dunsfold, Surrey, on the evening of 21 August 1974 to watch the Hawk's maiden flight would have imagined that the latest Hawker design would still be in production more than 40 years later. In those intervening years, more than 1,000 Hawks have been delivered and new developments of the design are still in train.

XX154, the first Hawk took to the air for a 53-minute flight before landing at dusk. The first flight routine was typically cautious but the handling proved fine with no untoward difficulties and a second flight was made the following afternoon.

The origins of the Hawk

The RAF's specification for a Jet Provost replacement had required a subsonic, single-engined, tandem-seat aircraft with a raised rear seat for the instructor. Both the British Aircraft Corporation (BAC) and

⌃ The first Hawk is still in service and flying with the Empire Test Pilots School at Boscombe Down. Here it is at Fairford in July 2015. *(Author)*

Hawker Siddeley Aviation (HSA) bid strongly for the contract as there was a potentially large order to the magnitude of 180 aircraft in the offing. HSA won the contract in October 1971 with its low-wing P1182 design powered by the Rolls-Royce/Turbomeca Adour and received a fixed price contract for 176 aircraft including a prototype. In August 1973 the RAF officially named the new trainer the 'Hawk'.

Flight test

The manufacturers were anxious to exhibit their new aircraft at the forthcoming Farnborough Air Show so after its maiden flight, XX154 rapidly made seven more flights and then flew on each of the seven show days. The Hawk was then grounded for the installation of full test instrumentation which had been delayed to allow for the

▲ 88 Hawks were modified to carry the Sidewinder AIM-9L air-to-air missile in addition to the 30mm cannon and became Hawk T1As. Hawk T1As of No 151 Squadron (bottom) and No 63 Squadron (above). Both the Hawks have Sidewinders on the wing pylons and the upper aircraft has a 30mm cannon pod.
(BAE Systems)

Farnborough appearance. The following five aircraft of the six-strong development batch were each tasked with differing roles in the flight test programme.

The Hawk had some initial faults which were soon remedied. Test Pilot Duncan Simpson found himself in a very difficult situation when stalling at altitude with the flaps at 50º and the undercarriage up. The tailplane stalled and the aircraft descended rapidly - he only managed to recover by retracting the flaps. Removal of a length of flap vane adjusted the downwash over the tailplane tip and cured the tailplane stall. Good spinning characteristics are an absolute necessity for a training aircraft and in a month-long test programme, specially instrumented XX158 made 350 spins finding that in all configurations the Hawk could recover. The Hawk was also tested as a weapons training platform. It was

configured with two inboard wing pylons and a centre fuselage Aden gun pod for trials, firings were carried out from ground level up to 30,000ft and in turns as tight as 6g. The manufacturer also cleared the Hawk for Matra rocket firings and release and jettison of light bombs. The last two Hawk test aircraft, XX159 and XX160 flew only initial tests from Dunsfold before relocating to the A&AEE Boscombe Down for acceptance trials with the RAF.

The six test aircraft flew over 500 hours in the test programme and five of these were refurbished and delivered to the Air Force. The first aircraft, XX154 remained with the makers and was then based at Llanbedr to escort drones and unmanned aircraft. It is currently at Boscombe Down with the ETPS for test pilot training. The eighth Hawk built was company-funded demonstrator G-HAWK/ZA101 which made its maiden flight on 17 May 1976

➤

and then joined the test programme. G-HAWK differed from the standard Hawk as it was fitted with a comprehensive navigational suite, full dual controls and other refinements such as a braking parachute.

Hawk T1s Service with the RAF

The Hawk was released for service in October 1976 after a very successful trials programme at the A&AEE Boscombe Down which showed satisfaction with the Hawk as an advanced trainer, clearing all its specified performance targets. The first two production Hawks were delivered to RAF Valley, Anglesey, in November 1976 and deliveries increased steadily as the production rate reached four a month for RAF in early 1978. Hawks replaced Gnats and Hunters in the advanced training role at RAF Valley. Hawks were also allotted for weapons training at the at the TWU at RAF Brawdy, South Wales, and these carried a centre line gun pod and two underwing pylons. This reduction in types simplified the training process. The student pilots spent 160hr on Jet Provosts and then graduated to the Hawk for 130hr on Hawk before moving on to an operational conversion unit. In August 1979, the Government concerned at a gap in Britain's air defence, 88 Hawks were modified to carry the Sidewinder AIM-9L air-to-air missile in addition to the 30mm cannon for secondary airfield defence duties. These were redesignated as Hawk T1As. Hawks would be used for local air defence of airfields, piloted by instructors

> The first export customer for the Hawk was Finland which order 50 in 1976. In 1993 the Finns received seven more and 18 ex-Swiss Air Force Hawks 66s joined the fleet in 2007. The entire Finnish Hawk fleet is planned to serve until the mid-2030s. *(BAE SYSTEMS North West Heritage)*

from the weapons training unit at RAF Brawdy.

Red Arrows

For almost 40 years the Royal Air Force Aerobatic Team, the *Red Arrows*, has flown the BAE Hawk and the aircraft is synonymous with the team. The Hawks offered a major technological advance over the Gnat, not least with its fuel consumption 30% less than the Gnats and greater stability in formation. A definite aerobatic advance was the new type's very good aileron control and the facility for 30sec of inverted flight, not possible with the Gnat. *The Red Arrows* are a household name, performing acrobatic manoeuvres of great skill and daring and wowing the crowds throughout the United Kingdom and many other countries. They represent both the prowess of the team and the excellence of the Hawk.

▼ The Red Arrows have operated the Hawk for 38 years and continue to excite crowds at air displays around the world. *(BAE Systems)*

Hawks for export

The Hawk was designed from the outset to be attractive to overseas market not only as a trainer but as a fighter/ground-attack aircraft. As part of the expansion of this aspect of the Hawk, G-HAWK was employed in trialling and expanding the Hawk's armament capabilities for fighter and ground attack roles. The manufacturer and Ministry of Defence recognised that licence production, offsets, finance deals and political manoeuvring would be necessary to clinch export sales.

The first export customer for the Hawk was Finland and in November 1976 their Defence Ministry announced an order for 50 Hawks to be delivered in 1979. Following four British-built aircraft, 46 were assembled by Patria in Finland. In 1993 the Finns received an additional seven Hawk 51As and 18 former Swiss Air Force Hawks 66s joined the fleet in 2007. The entire Finnish Hawk fleet including 24 with upgraded cockpits is prepared to serve until the mid-2030s. Selling aircraft in an overcrowded market was and is a matter of who can offer the best terms. Licenced production was a fact of life in aircraft sales and off-loaded the production facilities of the parent company. The Finnish company also manufactured some parts, such as the airbrake, from materials supplied by British Aerospace. Other customers soon followed Finland's lead. Kenya ordered twelve and Indonesia, which ordered eight and later bought 30 more. These three customers were the only recipients

▲ The Swiss received 20 Hawks. The first Swiss Hawk was built in the UK; the remainder were assembled at the Swiss Air Force base at Emmen. The 18 remaining were sold to Finland in 2007. *(BAE Systems)*

of the Hawk 50s which were very similar to the Hawk T1. The Hawk 50 was superseded by the Hawk 60 which became the standard export version. It was powered by the Adour 861, producing 10% more thrust at altitude and 20% more at low level. The maximum lift of the wing was increased and the flap mechanism modified to allow full-flap take-offs to reduce the take-off distance.

During 1980s orders continued to roll in from around the world. Zimbabwe was the first customer for the Hawk 60 buying eight and more orders came from Dubai, Abu Dhabi, Kuwait, Saudi Arabia and Switzerland. These 20 Swiss Hawks replaced elderly DH Vampires and whereas the first Swiss Hawk was built in the UK; the remainder were assembled at ➤

US Navy Goshawk about to touch down on the deck of a US aircraft carrier, with its leading-edge slats, airbrakes and arrestor hook out. *(BAE SYSTEMS North West Heritage)*

The first production Hawk 200 was ZJ201 which flew from Warton in February 1992. The only customers for the single-seat Hawk 200 have been Malaysia and Oman. *(BAE Systems)*

the Swiss Air Force base at Emmen in Kanton Luzern. (The 18 remaining Swiss aircraft were sold to Finland in 2007.) The final customer for the Hawk 60 was the Korean Air Force which ordered 20 examples which were hybrid aircraft, receiving some elements of the Hawk 200 including the lengthened nose.

The Hawk becomes the Goshawk

In 1979 the United States Navy formulated a requirement for jet trainer that could operate from its aircraft carriers. British Aerospace received a US Navy contract to develop a proposal for a navalised Hawk to replace the USN's Buckeye and Skyhawk. For this much tougher task, BAe's naval Hawk needed a strengthened undercarriage, a twin nosewheel, an arrestor hook and new avionics including a head-up display were required.

As BAe and McDonnell Douglas were already working closely together on the Harrier which served with the US Marine Corps they agreed to work in unison on this contract. They offered two different aircraft to the USN; the D-7000 and the Hawk, whichever aircraft was selected BAe would be the major sub-contractor. To help promote the Hawk, BAe's demonstrator G-HAWK was dispatched to USN bases for a month-long tour during

▲ Hawk 100 Demonstrator ZJ100. This was the first fully-representative Series 100 Hawk prototype and was the 359th Hawk built. It flew in October 1991 at Warton. *(BAE SYSTEMS North West Heritage)*

Improved Hawk for two - the Hawk 100

Launched in 1982, the two-seat Hawk 100 was an enhanced ground attack/advanced training aircraft equipped with inertial navigation, head-up display and weapons-aiming computer, optional laser or FLIR, and improved cockpit controls and displays, all linked by 1553B digital databus. External load was increased to 3,265kg. It introduced major aerodynamic improvements; the much-improved Combat Wing incorporating a slightly larger leading-edge radius and a very small amount of leading-edge droop, together a heightened fin with a RWR fairing and smurfs ahead of the tailplane which allowed the reinstatement of the full width double-slotted flaps. It also received aft-fuselage strakes which gave a 5-10% increase in take-off lift and helped to stabilise the aircraft for weapon aiming. It had a lengthened nose to incorporate a superior weapon avionics and the number of stores attachments was increased to seven and optional wingtip missile launch rails, which were specified by some customers.

Hawk development machine G-HAWK/ZA101 become the aerodynamic prototype for the Hawk 100 and flew in October 1987. It was not a Series 100 prototype in full, as the longer nose was mocked up out of alloy and plywood and it was only capable of carrying Series 50 avionics. The first fully-representative Series 100 Hawk prototype was ZJ100 which was the 359th Hawk built and flew in October 1991 at Warton. The first order for the 100 came from Abu Dhabi with an order for

18, the first of which were received in 1993 and others followed from Oman which ordered 30. More orders followed from Malaysia, Indonesia, Canada and Bahrain.

Single-seat Hawk 200

The single-seat version of the Hawk was planned by HSA in 1975 but only developed by British Aerospace nine years later. In the 100/200 series BAe managed to maintain the impressive 6,800lb carrying capacity on seven weapons stations while updating the leading and trailing edges of the wing to increase lift. The new aircraft had a 30% increase in lift through most of the flight envelope, and particularly in the combat areas.

The single-seater had a totally new nose section and repositioned nose wheel but in all other respects it aerodynamically represented the Hawk 100. The manufacturer envisaged that with its radar's air-to-air and air-to-surface modes it had a comprehensive range of roles, including airspace denial, close air support, battlefield interdiction, photo-reconnaissance and anti-shipping strike. The aircraft had some 80% airframe commonality with the two-seat Hawk 100 and was powered by an uprated, 26kN Adour 871 optimised for hot ambient conditions. It had an internal armament of two 25mm or 30mm Aden guns in a new front fuselage. The redesigned nose could also house a laser rangefinder, FLIR sensor or a multimode radar.

The Hawk 200 would have a loiter time of about four hours, 100 miles from base. The logic was that an air force could

which it carried a total of 86 guest pilots. Despite stiff competition the Hawk was selected by the US Navy and the contract was awarded to McDonnell Douglas as prime contractor, with BAe as major sub-contractor. The new aircraft was designated as the T-45 and later became the Goshawk.

When evaluating the three YT-45As test Goshawks, the USN identified major deficiencies, a high stalling speed, insufficient thrust, and poor stability in various flight configurations. To counter these adverse characteristics, airbrake operation was improved, the fin extended, nosewheel undercarriage doors closed after extension and the Adour's thrust increased. Even these modifications did not assuage the Navy dissatisfaction, so a full-span wing leading edge slat was introduced and a small horizontal fin, positioned in front of the tailplane allowing an increase in the size of the flaps.

The Goshawk became a radically different aircraft to the Hawk, needing costly, time-consuming modifications. Though the US Navy's original order for over 300 was whittled down to only 187 by budget cuts, it was still a sizeable fillip for the BAe Samlesbury and Brough factories which shared the sub-contract production for the USN Goshawk.

▲ **A Malaysian Hawk 108 and two single-seat Hawk 208s.** *(BAE Systems)*

put four small, cheap aircraft on patrol for the same price as one large sophisticated type, presenting a powerful threat to an invader.

The first Hawk 200, ZG200 made its maiden flight from Dunsfold on 19 May 1986 but crashed killing the pilot at Dunsfold only six weeks later. The second prototype ZH200 was already on the stocks and its production was expedited so it could fly on 24 April the following year. Despite the Hawk 200's multi-role ability only Indonesia, Malaysia and Oman purchased the aircraft, buying a total of 62 aircraft.

Building the Hawk

Final assembly and flight testing of the Hawk took place at Dunsfold with parts coming from Kingston and Brough. Between late 1979 and early 1982, 39 Hawks were assembled at Bitteswell, the last of these completing the RAF order. Complete production of the Hawk was passed to Brough after Kingston's closure in 1992 and these aircraft were then roaded to Warton for assembly and flight test. Between 2008 and 2010, Hawks made their maiden flights out of Brough to Warton. Several BAE programmes were axed in the 2010 Strategic Defence Review so Hawk

⌃ **BAE's Hawk 120 demonstrator ZJ951 which first flew in August 2002. The Hawk 120 had a new wing, forward and centre fuselage, fin and tailplane.** *(BAE Systems)*

production was transferred to Warton, with Brough reduced to technical support.

The current model – the Hawk 120

The Hawk 120 has less than 10% commonality with the previous marks. It has a new wing, forward and centre fuselage, fin and tailplane. In contrast to

the earlier models it has four times the fatigue life.

In recent years the Hawk has received large orders from the South African Air Force, the RAAF, the Indian Air Force, the RAF, the Omani and the Saudi Arabian Air Force. Offsets and licence production are still the name of the game and most of the RAAF aircraft were assembled in Australia.

India only received 24 from the UK

A pair of RAAF Hawk127s; A27-13 and A27-31. *(BAE Systems)*

RAF Hawk T2s ZK010 and ZK011 taking off.
(BAE Systems)

production line, with the remainder of their 66 aircraft order completed by Hindustan Aeronautics (HAL). In 2010 India increased its order by another 57 to 123 and in January 2017 HAL rolled out the 100th aircraft with indigenous-designed avionics refinements.

The RAF now has a fleet of 28 advanced T2s and 54 elderly T1s while the Royal Navy operates 13 T1s. The oldest examples operated by the UK are 39 years old. The first RAF Hawk

pre-production T2s ZK010 and ZK011 flew in 2004 and 2005 and the first production machine ZK012 in 2008. These Hawk T2 AJT (Advanced Jet Trainer) are very different to the T1. The latter has an analogue cockpit whereas the new aircraft have a modern digital glass cockpit and has embedded simulation and emulation technologies which to quote BAE Systems are, "capable of turning the skies into a hypothetical frontline warzone". The Hawk has a

datalink which can simulate threats from aircraft and weapons to which the pilot can respond by releasing virtual weapons.

In February 2016 BAE Systems signed a contract to supply the Royal Saudi Air Force with a second batch of 22 Hawk 165s (the export version of the AJT) in a commitment pushing the total orders for the jet trainer through the 1,000 barrier. Riyadh already had 22 of the new-generation Hawk trainers on order, the lead example of which made its maiden flight from Warton in September 2015. These 44 Hawk 165s will join 45 Hawk 65s and 65As. BAE's current backlog also includes eight Hawk 166s for Oman. These aircraft have the latest cockpit and training system modifications to help pilots from Saudi Arabia and Oman transition to the Eurofighter Typhoon. Thanks to these recent Saudi and Omani orders, production of Hawk AJTs is assured until 2018.

Advanced Hawk – launched 2017

In collaboration with Hindustan Aeronautics, BAE unveiled the Advanced Hawk at the Aero India show in Bangalore in February 2017. Development aircraft ZJ100 displayed the aircraft's new capabilities. The Advanced Hawk has active leading-edge slats and combat flaps on the wings and an enlarged display in the cockpit. It also features additional engine thrust, a laser designator pod, hardpoints that are smart-weapon enabled, a dual-purpose centre line pod (weapons or luggage),

▼ **The Hawk production line at BAE Warton.**
(BAE Systems)

In collaboration with Hindustan Aeronautics, BAE unveiled the Advanced Hawk at the Aero India show in Bangalore in February 2017. Remodelled Development aircraft ZJ100 displayed the new features including active leading-edge slats, combat flaps, air-to-air refuelling, defensive aids system, radar warning receiver and a digital head-up display. *(BAE Systems)*

air-to-air refuelling, defensive aids system including a countermeasures dispenser, radar warning receiver and a digital head-up display.

As the last remaining wholly British military aircraft programme, providing work for 1,900 in the UK, it has proved such a success, both at home and overseas, that if more orders can be assured that it will remain in production for many years to come. Sensibly the Hawk has been steadily improved during its forty-plus years of development; a whole series of very small steps, rather

Data	Hawk T2 AJT
Length	40ft 9in
Wingspan	32ft 7in
Height	13ft 1in
MTOW	16,480lbs
Max speed	630mph
Range	1,565mls
Crew	2
Powerplant	1 x Rolls-Royce Adour 951 6,800lbs

than a few giant leaps and this approach has paid dividends.

Saab – BAe Gripen

Following on from more than a decade of co-operation between the two companies, in 1995 British Aerospace signed an agreement with Saab to form Saab-BAe Gripen AB; a joint marketing, support and manufacturing agreement for an export variant of the Saab JAS39 Gripen.

The impetus for this agreement was BAe's research which had begun in 1980 into a lightweight, single-engined fighter. This failed to attract any UK official support so the agreement with Saab provided BAe Military Aircraft with a product which sat comfortably between the Hawk trainer and the Eurofighter Typhoon. In return Saab gained access to the global sales organization of British Aerospace which also adapted the capabilities of the Gripen to fit NATO standards and for flight refuelling.

BAe had been involved in the Gripen programme before 1995 and had designed and made the wings for the first three prototypes. In 1998 BAe purchased a 35% holding in Saab under which it would

produce 45% of the export Gripen airframes. The Brough, Yorkshire factory which was already building the Gripen main landing gear unit became the centre for Gripen manufacturing in the United Kingdom and was selected to assemble the wing attachment unit. The site was also responsible for the marrying-up these units and the subsequent connection of other assemblies. This resulted in the delivery from Brough of 77 complete Gripen centre fuselages for both single and two-seater variants.

A significant milestone for Saab-BAE SYSTEMS was achieved in December 1999 when the South African government ordered 28 Gripen fighters, including nine fully combat-capable two seaters. The order significantly also included 24 BAE Hawk 100 trainers. As part of an offset deal, Brough's Gripen work was gradually passed over to Denel in South Africa, initially by the manufacture at Brough of 22 kits and then wholesale manufacture by Denel.

In 2005 BAE reduced its stake in Saab to 20.5% in 2005 and in 2010 ended it, as it was concentrating its attention on the F-35. ∎

Saab Gripen demonstrator. For more than 15 years from 1995 BAE and Saab worked closely together to refine and market the Saab Gripen, which sat comfortably in the BAE portfolio between the Hawk trainer and the Typhoon. *(Saab)*

EAP to Eurofighter Typhoon

In the late 1970s BAe's project team at Warton began working on the fighter to replace the Lightning and the Phantom. Their objective was to produce an aircraft equal to the General Dynamics F-16 Fighting Falcon. In 1979 BAe and Messerschmitt-Bolkow-Blohm (MBB) agreed to work together on a new fighter design and devised the 'European Combat Fighter'. Then Dassault joined BAe and MBB and the project was renamed the 'European Combat Aircraft'.

This fell by the wayside but Warton's project engineers continued working on their designs and produced a smaller, cheaper version of the 'European Combat

▲ The all-British P110, a twin-engined delta with canards and a twin-fin mock-up was a BAe proposal for an aircraft to replace the Lightning and the Phantom.
(BAE SYSTEMS North West Heritage)

Aircraft', the all-British P.110, a twin-engined delta with canards and a twin-fin. This led to a design jointly produced by all the Panavia partners - the Agile Combat Aircraft (ACA) which was publicly displayed for the first time as a full-scale mock-up at Farnborough 1982. The ACA was relatively light, highly-manoeuvrable and capable of Mach 2. There was no official support for the ACA but on 26 May 1983 the Ministry of Defence placed a contract with BAe Warton to produce to produce a single experimental aircraft serialled ZF534 based on the ACA. It was to be funded 50:50 by the state and by industry.

The Jaguar FBW/ACT

As part of its preparation for the Lightning/Phantom replacement British Aerospace Warton had already been researching into the benefits of 'Fly by wire' (FBW) technology and relaxed stability. To trial these the MoD funded the conversion of a Sepecat Jaguar to prove them in flight. Originally built at Warton, Jaguar XX765 first flew in June 1975 and after brief service with the RAF was put into store at Abingdon twelve months after its maiden flight. It was reactivated and flown back to Warton in August 1978 for its extensive modification as a FBW trials machine.

▲ The P110 led to a design jointly produced by all the Tornado partners - the Agile Combat Aircraft (ACA) which was publicly displayed for the first time as a full-scale mock-up at Farnborough 1982. *(BAE SYSTEMS North West Heritage)*

On 20 October 1981 BAe's Chris Yeo made a world first when he piloted Jaguar S62 XX765 on its maiden flight as a fly-by-wire experimental aircraft. It used four independent computer-controlled electrical channels to relay instructions to the flight surfaces. It was the first aircraft ever to fly with its conventional control rod-controlled control surfaces entirely replaced by electrically signalled controls with no form of mechanical back-up. Any breakdown in the FBW control would have left the pilot with no other alternative than to have ejected.

From the start, the programme was an outstanding success. The FBW Jaguar was effortless to fly and handled superbly at incidences which normal Jaguars could not reach. Pilots commented on the lightness of the controls and the crispness of the response. In 1983 5cwt lead ballast was added in the tail to make the Jaguar unstable. Whereas aircraft had to be stable for a pilot to fly them, this natural stability worked against manoeuvring but with the addition of computers an unstable aircraft could be safely controlled.

Following its initial trials as an unstable aircraft it was then fitted with large wing leading-edge strakes, to further decrease longitudinal static stability. It was retitled the Jaguar ACT (Active Control Technology). It made its

first flight with these fitted in March 1984. To yet further increase the aircraft's instability, in July it was flown with destabilising ballast in fuel tanks on the inboard wing pylons. In this configuration XX765 was very unstable but the FBW systems enabled the pilot to indulge in

carefree handling, however hard he pulled the control column the aircraft never exceeded its flight envelope limits.

The Jaguar FBW/ACT made a total of 96 flights until its retirement in September 1984 and is now on display at the RAF Museum, Cosford.

▲ As part of the research for the new fighter the MoD funded the conversion of a Sepecat Jaguar to prove the benefits of 'Fly by wire' (FBW) technology and relaxed stability. Jaguar XX765 made its maiden flight as a 'Fly-by-wire' experimental aircraft. Note *'FBW'* on the fin. *(BAE SYSTEMS North West Heritage)*

Experimental Aircraft Programme

The Experimental Aircraft Programme (EAP) was built to demonstrate several recent developments for the first time. These included full authority digital fly-by-wire, and unstable canard delta configuration, electronic cockpit design, digital engine control, composite materials and stealth. Initially there were to be two EAPs, one each in Britain and Germany but in December 1983 the German the Italian governments withdrew support. Germany was to have built the centre and rear fuselage, but without its contribution the airframe was built by BAe at Warton and employed a Tornado rear fuselage and fin/rudder. Aeritalia invested some of its own funds to remain in the project, fabricating one of the carbon-fibre wings and BAe built the other. Equipment suppliers were eager to stay connected the project. Turbo-Union leant two RB199 engines and German and Italian firms donated equipment to the EAP; though more than half of the equipment suppliers were from the UK. Carbon fibre was used in the wing, foreplane, cockpit substructure and side panels, accounting for 25 per cent of the structure weight. If the two partner countries had not dropped out this proportion would have been even greater.

The EAP was a single-seat delta canard powered by two Turbo-Union RB199 with reheat each developing 17,000 lbs thrust as installed on the Tornado F3 interceptor but without their thrust reversers. The EAP's chin intake with a hinged lower lip which rotated

XX765 was flown with ballast as an unstable aircraft and was then fitted with large wing leading-edge strakes, to further decrease longitudinal stability. These yellow strakes are clearly seen in this photo prior to painting. It was retitled the Jaguar ACT (Active Control Technology). *(BAE SYSTEMS North West Heritage)*

down at slow speeds and higher angle of attack to improve flow into the engine. At higher speeds it moved up to minimise spillage drag.

The compound delta wing with its 57^0 sweep inboard and moderate 45^0 sweep outboard was 36ft 8in wide. There were 13 control surfaces, including camber changing leading edge slats and flaps to provide maximum lift in subsonic combat and minimum drag in supersonic flight. Pitch control was provided by the all-moving canard foreplane and trailing edge flaperons. Twin airbrakes were fitted on the upper rear fuselage. Because the EAP was 15% more unstable than the ACT Jaguar and with its plethora of control surfaces the flight computers operated at three times the speed of the Jaguar ACT. Overall length was 48ft 3in and the fuselage was area ruled to reduce drag, the nose was drooped to offer good visibility. Fuel was mainly carried in the wings but 14 smaller tanks were fitted in the fuselage.

In many respects the EAP was fundamentally different from its predecessors. Manufacturers no longer just developed the airframe leaving the remainder to sub-contractors; avionics is at the heart of the combat aircraft's capabilities and BAe brought that technology in-house.

⌃ XX765 flying with Tornado F2 ZD901. The large wing leading-edge strakes are now painted and the 'ACT' on the fin is for 'Active Control Technology'. *(BAE SYSTEMS North West Heritage)*

▲ The EAP (Experimental Aircraft Programme) ZF534 was built to demonstrate full authority digital fly-by-wire, unstable canard delta configuration, electronic cockpit design, digital engine control, composite materials and stealth. It made its maiden flight on 8 August 1986. *(BAE SYSTEMS North West Heritage)*

A stunning photo of ZF534 carrying the number 203 for its appearance in the flying display at the 1987 Paris Air Show. *(BAE SYSTEMS North West Heritage)*

Flight trials

Rolled out on 16 April 1986, the single EAP ZF534, piloted by Dave Eagles, made its maiden flight on 8 August and unusually for such an event reached Mach 1.1 at 30,000ft. It then achieved 20 flights in the subsequent 17 days and was cleared to Mach 1.4 and 39,000ft. Then it was flown to Farnborough where it impressed the crowds. The EAP's flight envelope was gradually expanded and in June the flowing year it was demonstrated at the Paris Air Show during which it made its 100th flight. On its return from France it was flown by MBB, Aeritalia and RAF pilots. David Eagles commented that the EAP was a delight to fly and with the addition of a weapons system would have been an excellent fighter.

In 1989 the EAP was fitted with a Eurofighter type single airbrake in support of its development. This was fixed and could only be altered when the aircraft was on the ground. It was tested at various incidences up to speeds of Mach 0.9. On 1 May 1991 ZF534 made its final flight and was stored at Warton. It had completed 259 test sorties totalling 195.21 flying hours, during which it had reached speeds of Mach 2.1 and angles of attack of over 35^0 in controlled flight. It is now on display at the RAF Museum Cosford.

The EAP proved an invaluable research tool which saved a considerable amount time and money which would otherwise

⌃ **The EAP flying low in front of the hangars at BAe Warton.** *(BAE SYSTEMS North West Heritage)*

have been directly expended on the Eurofighter programme.

The European Fighter Aircraft

In May 1983 five European nations; Britain, France, Italy, Spain and West Germany joined together to build a new Future European Fighter Aircraft (FEFA), to fulfil their national requirements from 1995 for an agile, single-seat, twin-engine air combat fighter. France demanded 50% work share, project leadership, flight testing and sales led from France with ancillary equipment selected by a French-controlled committee. Not surprisingly the other four partners rejected this stance and France left the partnership and developed the Dassault Rafale.

Some engineers in the UK felt that as early as 1978, British industry was ready to begin development of a new agile fighter to enter service in the late 1980s, and had gone as far as investing more than £100 million in a flying showcase for its fighter technology with the EAP. Instead of an all-British fighter, UK industry would have to make do with 33% of an admittedly larger four-nation European fighter aircraft programme.

British Aerospace, MBB, Aeritalia, and Casa formed the Munich based Eurofighter company in 1986 to manage the programme, with the work split 33:33:21:13 to match each country's share of the 765 aircraft planned. Similarly, Rolls-Royce, MTU, Fiat, and ITP established the Munich-based Eurojet to oversee development of the EJ200 engine required for EFA. No similar grouping was planned to direct development of EFA avionics and systems. Instead, Eurofighter assigned overall responsibility for avionics to British Aerospace, for flight controls to MBB, and for utilities to Aeritalia. In November 1988, the four partners signed a Development Phase contract for the airframe and engine and the production of nine prototypes including twin-seaters. Radar and Defensive Aids contracts followed in 1990 and 1992 respectively. Progress with the aircraft faltered badly after the end of the 'Cold War' came to an end in 1990. By 1992 Germany was faced with the huge costs of re-unification and the need for such a sophisticated fighter aircraft seemed less necessary and almost withdrew from the project. It is possible that if Germany had withdrawn that Italy and Spain would have followed suit. After considering other types such as the

⌃ The EAP played a part in Eurofighter development fitted with a Eurofighter style airbrake, requiring removal of part of the spine. This was fixed when in flight and could only be altered when the aircraft was on the ground. It was tested at 15, 30 and 45 degrees and tested at speeds up to Mach 0.9. *(BAE SYSTEMS North West Heritage)*

McDonnell Douglas Hornet, Germany decided that with £5bn already spent it on EFA was past the point of no return. Requirements were finalised for a slightly less costly New EFA (NEFA) renamed Eurofighter 2000 and development was agreed with the partner nations in 1996. Each company would have its own final assembly and flight test centre.

Benefitting from the successful development of the Jaguar ACT and the EAP, Eurofighter 2000 was defined as an extremely agile supersonic twin-engined single-seater able to super-cruise (i.e. fly supersonically without using reheat). It had a light airframe as only 15% was made from metal. It would have optimal performance for an air superiority role in beyond visual range and close combat, matched with a comprehensive air-to-ground attack capability.

In May 1990, the contract was agreed for the GEC-Marconi ECR90. Trials began January 1993 in BAC One-Eleven 475 ZE433 which had a specially extended nose to accommodate the ECR90 or Captor radar. Captor was then fitted to

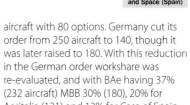

BAE Systems

Airbus Defence and Space (Germany)

Alenia Aermacchi

Airbus Defence and Space (Spain)

⌃ **The work share on the Eurofighter Typhoon programme. (Alenia Aermacchi is now called Leonardo.)** *(BAE SYSTEMS North West Heritage)*

DA3 and DA4 for trials.

In August 1996, the UK National Audit Office put the total cost of the programme to the UK at £15.4bn, with a unit production cost for 250 aircraft of £38m. In January 1998 production contracts were finally signed for 620

aircraft with 80 options. Germany cut its order from 250 aircraft to 140, though it was later raised to 180. With this reduction in the German order workshare was re-evaluated, and with BAe having 37% (232 aircraft) MBB 30% (180), 20% for Aeritalia (121) and 13% for Casa of Spain

➤

The first Eurofighter Development Aircraft DA1 98+29 assembled in Manching flew on 27 March 1994.
(Copyright Eurofighter)

(87). (BAe is now BAE SYSTEMS, Aeritalia is now Leonardo while MBB and CASA are now part of Airbus Defence & Space.)

All this prevarication had an adverse effect on the entry into service to Typhoon which would not now be until 2003. Even after that controversy was not escaped when Germany baulked at the name 'Typhoon' for Eurofighter as it reminded them of the highly effective Hawker Typhoons on World War 2.

BAE's share of Production

BAE has the largest share of the production of the aircraft and its Samlesbury factory manufactures the foreplanes, spine, front fuselage including the cockpit, fin, inboard flaperons, stage 1 of the rear fuselage, and wing to fuselage brackets. Final assembly is at the Warton plant's 302 hangar, previously the location for Tornado final assembly. UK flight testing is also centred at Warton. BAE is responsible for avionics which covers avionics integration, displays and controls, electromagnetic compatibility, integrated monitoring and recording system, lightning protection, electrical and fuel systems, defensive aids, escape and life support systems and direct voice input control.

Prototypes

Seven prototypes or development machines were built; designated as DA1-DA7, each with specially allotted test roles. Each country had two prototypes except Spain that only had one. Two of these prototypes; DA4 and DA6 were twin-seaters. Clearly seven development aircraft would be insufficient for the flight test tasking so five of the initial production aircraft, IPA1 – IPA5 were fitted out with test instrumentation. Three further initial production aircraft joined these as IPA6-1PA8 and five instrument production aircraft ISPA1-ISPA5 kitted out with test equipment to record performance in service. A total of 20 instrumented aircraft.

⌃ BAe's Development Aircraft DA2 ZH588 taking off on its first flight at Warton on 4th April 1994.
(Copyright Eurofighter - Geoffrey Lee)

➤ BAE DA2 ZH588 at Farnborough 2002. The aircraft is carrying two 'smokewinders' and four AMRAAM missiles.
(Copyright Eurofighter - Geoffrey Lee)

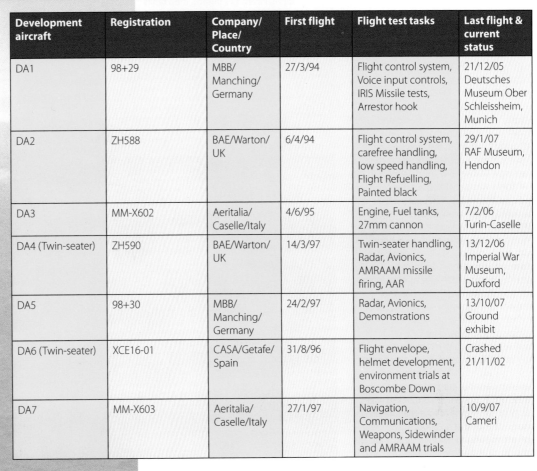

Development aircraft	Registration	Company/ Place/ Country	First flight	Flight test tasks	Last flight & current status
DA1	98+29	MBB/ Manching/ Germany	27/3/94	Flight control system, Voice input controls, IRIS Missile tests, Arrestor hook	21/12/05 Deutsches Museum Ober Schleissheim, Munich
DA2	ZH588	BAE/Warton/ UK	6/4/94	Flight control system, carefree handling, low speed handling, Flight Refuelling, Painted black	29/1/07 RAF Museum, Hendon
DA3	MM-X602	Aeritalia/ Caselle/Italy	4/6/95	Engine, Fuel tanks, 27mm cannon	7/2/06 Turin-Caselle
DA4 (Twin-seater)	ZH590	BAE/Warton/ UK	14/3/97	Twin-seater handling, Radar, Avionics, AMRAAM missile firing, AAR	13/12/06 Imperial War Museum, Duxford
DA5	98+30	MBB/ Manching/ Germany	24/2/97	Radar, Avionics, Demonstrations	13/10/07 Ground exhibit
DA6 (Twin-seater)	XCE16-01	CASA/Getafe/ Spain	31/8/96	Flight envelope, helmet development, environment trials at Boscombe Down	Crashed 21/11/02
DA7	MM-X603	Aeritalia/ Caselle/Italy	27/1/97	Navigation, Communications, Weapons, Sidewinder and AMRAAM trials	10/9/07 Cameri

The first two prototypes flew within a fortnight of each other. DA1 98+29 was piloted by Peter Weger on 27 March from MBB's plant at Manching and Chris Yeo took DA2 ZH588 into the air from Warton on 6 April 1994. It had been planned that DA1 would make 20 flights from Manching and the transfer to Warton where it would receive the UK military registration ZH586 and continue testing from there. Not surprisingly this proposal was dropped and DA1 remained in Germany.

Neither of the first two aircraft were fitted with radar or the EJ200 engine and initially flew with the RB199 that was fitted to the Tornado. All subsequent Eurofighters had the EJ200 and DA1 and DA2 received the EJ200 engines in 1996 and 1998 respectively. DA1 made the type's first public display at the ILA Berlin in May 1996 with DA2 appearing at the Farnborough Air Show later the same year. In June 2000 ZH588 was repainted all-black, when 490 pressure transducers were attached to its right side to measure

▲ BAE SYSTEMS DA4 ZH590 with drop tanks during air-to-air refuelling trials with VC10 K4 ZD242 over the North Sea. (BAE SYSTEMS North West Heritage)

the effects on the carbon fibre structure in high 'g' manoeuvres. In 2006 it took part in asymmetric store carriage handling trials for which an anti-spin parachute was installed in case the aircraft departed from normal flight.

Though still without radar, the first Eurofighter to fly with the dedicated EJ200 engine was the Italian's DA3 in June 1995. Naturally DA3's main task was engine development. Another task was testing the single Mauser BK27mm cannon. In the RAF there was debate about the need for the cannon but the other partners all favoured its inclusion. To save money the RAF even entertained the idea of only equipping only its Tranche 1 Typhoons with the gun and installing ballast in it is place in to the remaining Tranche 2 and 3 aircraft. Recent experience in Afghanistan and Iraq showed that guns had their uses so thankfully common sense prevailed and all the fleet are to receive the cannon.

Spain's sole prototype DA6, a twin-seater, was the next in the air in August 1996. It was employed on flight envelope expansion and helmet development but crashed after a double flame-out in November 2002. DA6 was carrying out engine relight trials when one engine died at 40,000ft, as the crew was attempting to relight it at 30,000ft the other engine died. As it was a development aircraft it did not have a Ram-Air-Turbine installed which if deployed would provide hydraulic and electrical power. In an unstable aircraft loss of power makes the aircraft uncontrollable, so the crew ejected.

The remaining three development batch machines made the maiden flights

Eurofighter IPA3 98+03 carrying IRIS-T, Paveway 2 bombs, drop tanks and AMRAAM missiles over Bavaria.
(Copyright Eurofighter - Geoffrey Lee)

in quick succession in the space of seven weeks in early 1997. The last to take to the air was BAE's twin-seater ZH590 in mid-March.

Instrumented Production Aircraft

The initial production by the four-nation grouping was for a tranche of 148 machines completed in April 2008. This tranche was divided into two batches and these were batches were themselves sub-divided into three (Block 1, 1B and 1C) and four blocks (Blocks 2, 2b, 5 and 5A) respectively, each block gradually introducing better standards of software. Eventually all Tranche 1 aircraft were brought up to Block 5 standard which updated the existing air defence capability by conferring full 9G operability and full air-to-ground weapons capability. Often wrongly regarded as a narrow-specification Cold War bomber-destroyer, Typhoon was always intended to be a swing-role machine, carrying out air-to-air and air-to-ground operations with equal facility – and indeed 'swinging' from one role to the other during the same mission, at the flick of a switch. For the RAF the Eurofighter was always viewed as a Jaguar fighter-bomber replacement, as well as a replacement for Tornado and Phantom air defence fighters.

⌃ **Italian Eurofighter DA7 MM-X603 in a loop.** *(Copyright Eurofighter)*

Tranche 2 deliveries began to the partner nations in late 2008. These aircraft had; a strengthened undercarriage and fuselage for carrying heavier weapons, front fuselage modifications to facilitate future radar and sensor updates and new mission computers providing the level of processing and memory needed for the sophisticated weapons within the aircraft's armoury.

Following on from the development aircraft and built as part of the first tranche of production aircraft, the first five IPAs (Instrumented Production Aircraft) are heavily involved in the development programme, most particularly the radar, flight refuelling and air-to-ground capability. These were numbered IPA1-IPA5 and just like the DA batch these aircraft did not fly in numerical order. Three flew in April 2002; Italian-assembled IPA2 MM.X614 was the first in the air from Turin-Caselle on 5th April, next came EADS IPA3 98+03 on 8th April and the first British-assembled production aircraft IPA1 followed seven days later from Warton. IPA1 is supporting drop tests from Warton, IPA2 is currently engaged in the integration of the deep strike MBDA Storm Shadow missile. This builds on the ground trials of the weapon and two successful releases of Storm Shadow from Italian IPA2 in 2015. In addition, further firing trials have been completed with MBDA's Meteor Beyond Visual Range Air-to-Air missile. The sixth in a series of firings completed ▶

▼ **Typhoon production line at Warton in 2004. Tranche 1 aircraft in production for the RAF with ZJ802 on the extreme left**.
(BAE Systems)

TYPHOON
A PHASED APPROACH TO DEVELOPMENT

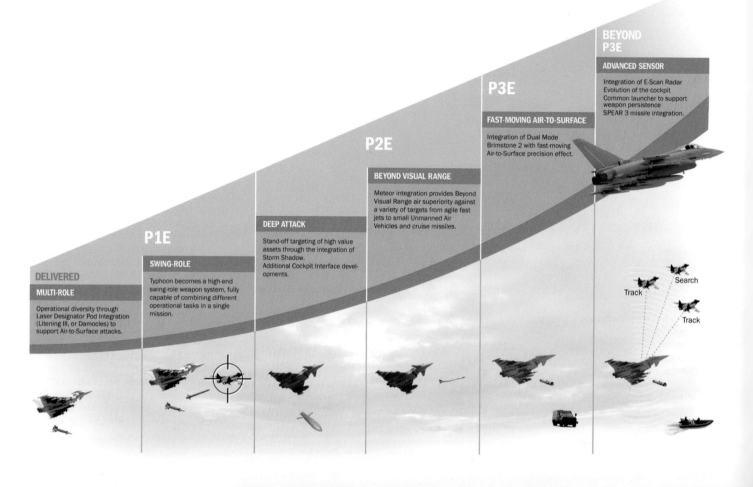

BEYOND P3E

ADVANCED SENSOR

Integration of E-Scan Radar
Evolution of the cockpit
Common launcher to support
weapon persistence
SPEAR 3 missile integration.

P3E

FAST-MOVING AIR-TO-SURFACE

Integration of Dual Mode
Brimstone 2 with fast-moving
Air-to-Surface precision effect.

P2E

BEYOND VISUAL RANGE

Meteor integration provides Beyond
Visual Range air superiority against
a variety of targets from agile fast
jets to small Unmanned Air
Vehicles and cruise missiles.

DEEP ATTACK

Stand-off targeting of high value
assets through the integration of
Storm Shadow.
Additional Cockpit Interface developments.

P1E

SWING-ROLE

Typhoon becomes a high-end
swing-role weapon system, fully
capable of combining different
operational tasks in a single
mission.

DELIVERED

MULTI-ROLE

Operational diversity through
Laser Designator Pod Integration
(Litening III, or Damocles) to
support Air-to-Surface attacks.

Search

Track

Track

by IPA2 using the UK's Hebrides range in 2016, were intended to continue to expand the clearance envelope of the weapon. As Typhoon is an aerodynamically unstable aircraft unlike Tornado, it is very sensitive to additional shapes and loads which may impinge upon the flight control system ability to maintain stability.

Germany's IPA3 98+03 was used for under-wing load tests. Casa's IPA4 C.16-20 is now testing Weapons System Performance and Communications. Warton-assembled IPA5 ZJ700 was tasked with handling and transonic tests and in July 2016 started trialling the developed Captor-E radar.

The first Tranche 2 aircraft was German single-seater 98+07 designated as IPA7 was tasked with achieving clearance for that variant. IPA 6 ZJ938's most recent tasks have been flight trials with the Air-to-Surface MBDA Brimstone precision strike missile ahead of firing trials as part of a programme of work to integrate the weapon with the aircraft. The final Instrumented Production Aircraft, IPA8 98+08 took to the air on 12th September 2016 and will join BAE's IPA5 trialling the Captor-E radar.

Five Typhoons were also specially instrumented for trials and onward delivery to their air forces. Two were built

▲ ZJ699 in Tranche 3e configuration with four Meteor BVRAAM missiles, two Brimstone 2 precision strike weapons (each comprising 3 missiles), two ASRAAM missiles and two Paveway IV laser guided precision weapons. Typhoon FGR4 ZK356 was displayed in this configuration at RIAT 2016, and the Farnborough International Air Show 2016. *(BAE SYSTEMS)*

for these roles by both BAE and Leonardo and one by Casa.

Tranche 3 Production

On 31st July 2009 owing to financial constraints the four partner nations agreed to split the Tranche 3 contract into two. They then signed the Tranche 3A production contract for 112 aircraft, worth €9 billion. This number comprises 40 for the UK, 31 for Germany, and 21 for Italy and 20 for Spain. Tranche 3B is very unlikely to go ahead so the total Typhoon fleet for the four will be 472. However there have been substantial orders from other countries; namely Austria, Saudi Arabia, Oman and most recently Kuwait.

Tranche 3 models physically differ little from the previous aircraft. The aircraft has some small panels on the fuselage to accommodate the fitting of Conformal Fuel Tanks. There is a new internal structure in the nose section designed to accommodate the wirings, power, cooling and electronics for the new E-Scan radar. Tranche 3 aircraft also feature Hi-speed Data Networking capabilities and more computing power.

In September 2011 BAE Systems revealed that the annual Typhoon production rate was to be reduced significantly. Four final assembly sites around Europe were configured to

▲ Italian IPA2 MM.X614 taking off from Warton during Storm Shadow dropping trials in September 2015. Storm Shadow is under the right wing and a camera pod under the fuselage.
(BAE SYSTEMS)

deliver up to a combined 60 Typhoons a year, with 53 planned in 2011, but production fell to 43 a year by late 2012, before later being reduced further to 35. In November 2015 the production rate was halved to keep the line open until 2020. The decision to extend the production schedule enables the Eurofighter consortium to keep its final assembly lines active while it pursues international sales opportunities.

Typhoon's Performance

The Eurojet EJ200 engines have proved to offer excellent combat thrust-to-weight ratio in excess of 1.2:1. Besides conferring on the aircraft the ability to supercruise, (i.e. fly supersonically without using reheat) engines enable the aircraft to go supersonic in under 30 seconds and to reach M1.6 at 36,000ft less than 2.5 minutes after take-off. It can also fly at Mach 2 at up to 65,000ft. The Typhoon's

RAF Nos 3(F) and 29(R) Squadron single-seat Typhoons based at RAF Coningsby, Lincolnshire. *(Copyright Eurofighter - Geoffrey Lee)*

Flight Control System enable the pilot to fly aggressively to out manoeuvre opposition.

It is an agile, multi/swing-role aircraft equipped with 13 hardpoints to carry a mix of ordnance and fuel. Its comprehensive sensors facilitate the use of weapons for air-to-air and air-to-ground operations. It has a full glass cockpit, with head-up and head-down displays, all-round vision and utilises a unique Helmet Mounted Symbology System (HMSS). The HMSS provides flight reference and weapon data aiming through the visor. Other features such as Direct Voice Input and Hands on Throttle And Stick (HOTAS) control functions have been implemented on the Eurofighter Typhoon to drastically reduce the pilot's workload. Voice + Throttle and Stick (VTAS) enables single pilot operations even in the most demanding situations.

Eurofighter Typhoon is at the forefront of sensor fusion technology and the sensor suite continues to be upgraded to deliver enhanced detection and decision-making. Combining the data from key sensors gives the pilot an autonomous ability to rapidly assess the overall tactical situation and respond efficiently to identified threats.

Further improvements

In November 2016 the three Typhoons assigned to the RAF's 41(R) Test and Evaluation Squadron based at Coningsby began trials of Typhoon modified to

German Air Force Typhoon of JG-74.
(Copyright Eurofighter)

◄ No 11 Squadron RAF Typhoon at Green Flag, USA. The Typhoon is loaded with Paveway 2 bombs, Litening designater pod and drop tanks.
(Copyright Eurofighter - Geoffrey Lee)

with this weapons fit, it lost none of its incredible agility and manoeuvreability. Development beyond P3E would be the integration of the new Captor-E Active Electronically Scanned Array radar ensuring that Typhoon could continue to operate in hostile environments in the future.

Sales

As Typhoon is a shared project, markets for sales are also shared out between the partner countries. BAE was given responsibility for Australia, Bahrain, Canada, Indonesia, Malaysia, Saudi Arabia, Singapore and UAE, countries where it had been successful in selling military aircraft. Most of them are currently BAE Hawk operators. BAE and its predecessor companies had a long relationship with Saudi Arabia in particular and has provided aircraft and trained crews for it. As an incentive to each of the partners where sales are achieved in one of their specific markets, final assembly then takes place at their factory, though parts continue to be drawn in from the consortium.

By April 2017, 500 Typhoons had been delivered, from a total order book of 599. Eurofighter delivered a combined total of 47 Typhoons over the 12-month period to the end of May 2016. Besides the four partner nations Typhoon has received orders from Austria, Saudi Arabia, Oman and Kuwait. Based on current commitments, final assembly lines in Germany and Spain have work until the end of 2018, while those in Italy and the UK – which respectively led sales campaigns in Kuwait and Oman, will run on until 2020. With the likelihood of production lines closing partner companies have stepped up their efforts to secure additional export orders.

In 2002 Austria placed an order for 18 Tranche 2 aircraft, though in the event it received 15 Tranche 1 Typhoons from the production line at Manching. With BAE's close ties with Saudi Arabia, supplying

Phase 1 Enhancements Further Work(P1EbFW) standard. With this fit the aircraft takes on a Swing-role capability, combining different operational tasks within a single mission. This is the first phase of Project Centurion which will eventually lead to a P2E standard which will allow the Typhoon to take over the ground-attack role of the Tornado GR4 as they are retired from service at the end of 2018. Under P2E enhancements initial integration of MBDA's Meteor beyond visual range air-to-air missile and the Storm Shadow stand-off air-to-surface missiles will be carried out. P2E aircraft will also incorporate software and avionics improvements to the radar, defensive aids systems and targeting pods. These enhancements will not only increase threat awareness and pilot safety, but also improve Typhoon's targeting capabilities.

Phase 3 Enhancements

The Phase 3 Enhancement Programme will enable Eurofighter operators to integrate the Brimstone 2 on the aircraft and will also further enhance other existing weapons capabilities, including Storm Shadow, Meteor, Paveway IV and ASRAAM. The P3E standard is due to be delivered in 2017. It will further enable the Typhoon to deploy several more capabilities including precision-guided air-to-surface weapons at fast-moving targets with low-collateral damage. So by 2019, Typhoon will be fulfilling a number

of roles including air defence of the UK, stand-off attack and close air support, able to switch roles without having to reconfigure its weapons. A truly multi-role aircraft.

BAE demonstrated a Typhoon Tranche 3 in the Phase 3 Enhancement configuration at the 2016 Fairford RIAT and at the Farnborough Air Show. Though loaded with six Brimstones, four Meteors and two Paveway precision-guided bombs the Typhoon showed that even

▼ Austrian Air Force Typhoon 7L-WH.
(Copyright Eurofighter - Markus Zinner)

Hunters, Lightnings, Strikemasters, Tornadoes and Hawks an order from it for the Typhoon was far from surprising. An order came from Saudi Arabia for 72 aircraft came in 2006 to be delivered from the Warton production line and 66 of these had been delivered by the end of 2016. There has long been talk of more orders for the Typhoon from Saudi Arabia and the effectiveness of Typhoon in airstrikes against Yemeni and Islamic State insurgents appeared to be giving BAE Systems increasing confidence that it will receive more orders from that source soon. Eurofighter made a very strong sales pitch in India but after a long period of uncertainty the Indians ordered the French-built Rafale. In December 2012, after a six-year gap in any export orders, Oman became the aircraft's seventh customer and ordered a total of twelve aircraft for delivery from the British assembly line. In April 2015 there was a strong fillip to the sales programme when Kuwait ordered 28 Tranche 3 aircraft, these to be delivered from the Italian plant at Caselle, Turin from 2019.

In service

The Royal Air Force established its first operational Typhoon squadrons at Coningsby, Lincolnshire, in 2004, with a subsequent squadron at Leuchars, Fife, in 2008. These initial aircraft were designated as T1s which are Tranche 1, batch 1 twin-seat trainers while Typhoon T1As are Tranche 1, batch 2 two-seat trainers. The F2 is the single-seat fighter variant. The RAF's Typhoon force was declared operational in the air defence role on 21 June 2007, when the aircraft started taking on the Quick Reaction Alert

(QRA) commitment, maintaining aircraft at 24/7 readiness to counter threats to the UK's air space armed with AMRAAM/ASRAAM (Advanced medium-/short-range air-to-air missiles).

Owing to the need to deploy Typhoon to 'Operation Herrick' in Afghanistan 2008, urgent UK-only work was conducted on Tranche 1 Block 5 aircraft to develop an air-to-ground capability. These aircraft were built as new or upgraded from F2s and were declared as multi-role in July 2008, gaining the designation FGR4 for the single seat version or T3 for the twin-seater. They can carry the Litening Laser Designator Pod and Paveway 2, Enhanced Paveway 2 and 1000lb freefall bomb. The RAF's FGR4s became operational in the air-to-ground role on 1 July 2008.

Other squadrons are based as follows; RAF Coningsby, Lincolnshire, houses No. 3 Squadron; No. 11 Squadron; No. 29 Squadron, OCU Tactical pilot training and evaluation; and No. 41 Test & Evaluation Squadron. RAF Lossiemouth, Moray, Scotland houses No. 1 Squadron; No. 2 Squadron and No. 6 Squadron. RAF Mount Pleasant, East Falkland, Falkland Islands, houses No. 1435 Flight where the Typhoon took over the Islands air defence from Tornado F3s in September 2009. Six Typhoons were based in Italy during 'Operation Ellamy' against Libya, four of which operated in the ground attack role. In the following year four aircraft were based at RAF Northolt to provide immediate air defence during the London Olympics.

The RAF is the largest Eurofighter

Typhoon customer and its 140th aircraft was delivered in December 2016. It is receiving 40 Tranche 3A aircraft to supplement its 53 Tranche 1 giving a total of 160 when deliveries are completed. It was planned that the Tranche 1 aircraft would be retired in 2018, but in November 2015 the UK Government announced that it would extend the life of the multi-role Typhoon for 10 extra years up to 2040 and would be able to create 2 additional squadrons. This would provide a total of 7 front line squadrons, consisting of approximately 12 aircraft per squadron.

The Luftwaffe received 35 Tranche 1 aircraft with the final delivery in 2008 which were subsequently modified to Block 5 standard. The Tranche 1 aircraft were joined by 77 Tranche 2 Eurofighters, and from Tranche 3A production the Germans will receive 31 aircraft. The Tranche 3B orders were cancelled by the German Government so with its last delivery in 2018 the Luftwaffe will have a total fleet of 140 Eurofighters. The Luftwaffe's aircraft are divided into three tactical air wings and employed in the air defence role, though Germany is now considering expanding the aircraft's role and adopting some of the RAF's Typhoons capabilities.

In what proved to be a very politically controversial move, in 2001 Austria ordered 30 Typhoons including six two-seat trainers. Budgetary

considerations resulted in this was being whittled down to 15 Tranche 1 single-seaters, all delivered from the Manching production line. The first aircraft was delivered in 2007 and the aircraft were in service in the air-defence role strictly within Austria's borders two years later.

The Eurofighter project ran so far behind schedule that it caused Italy's Aeronautica Militaire Italia (AMI) severe problems with resourcing its air defence fleet. So much so that it upgraded 60 of it elderly Lockheed Super Starfighter F-104s and leased 24 Tornado F3s from the RAF from 1995 until 2004. The AMI received the first of its 27 Tranche 1 aircraft in February 2004 when the first aircraft was delivered and final delivery was in February 2008. The Typhoons began operating in the air-defence role Quick Reaction Alert (QRA) role at the end of 2005 ahead of the other partner nations. Besides the interceptor role, the AMI is developing the mission capability of its Typhoons even further. By September 2012 these Tranche 1 aircraft had been modified to Block 5 standard. Following on from these were 47 Tranche 2 aircraft. The AMI is receiving 21 Tranche 3A aircraft and the first delivery of this version was in mid-2014.

The Spanish Air Force accepted its first Typhoon in September 2003 and the first squadron began equipping with the type in the following year. It originally ordered

Data	EAP	Typhoon
Length	48ft 3in	52ft 4in
Wingspan	38ft 7in	38ft 7in
Height	18ft 2in	17ft 49in
MTOW	32,000lbs	51,800lbs
Max speed	M2 at altitude	M2 at altitude
Combat range	n.a.	Air defence with 3 hour loiter 100nm Ground attack 750nm
Crew	1	1/2
Engine	2 × RB199-104D 9,000lb dry / 17,000lb reheat	2 × Eurojet EJ200 afterburning turbofan 13,500lbs dry / 20,200lbs reheat Mauser 27mm cannon
Armament		AMRAAM, ASRAAM, Meteor, Maverick, Harm, Brimstone, Storm Shadow, Paveway, Drop tanks

87 aircraft, of which 60 have been delivered as of December 2015. 20 of its aircraft are from Tranche 1, 33 in Tranche 2 and 20 in Tranche 3A.

In December 2005, the order for 72 Typhoons was announced for the Saudi Arabian Air Force. The first 40 were Tranche 2 aircraft, the remainder Tranche 3A. Deliveries of these aircraft from Warton are nearing completion but BAE

and the Saudi Government have long been negotiating and order for more Typhoons, which may materialise.

Not only has Typhoon has proved a profitable investment for BAE SYSTEMS, maintaining the technological prowess of the company and providing work for 5,000 of its staff but it has also provided air forces with a state-of-the-art weapons system. ∎

Two RSAF Typhoon Trainers 321 and 322 waiting to take off at Warton. They are carrying UK military serials ZK088 and ZK089. They were delivered in April 2013. *(BAE SYSTEMS)*

1 Glass reinforced plastic radome, hinged to starboard for access
2 GEC Marconi Avionics ECR-90 Captor multi-mode pulse-Doppler radar scanner
3 Scanner actuating mechanism
4 Radome hinge
5 Radar mounting bulkhead
6 Retractable flight refuelling probe
7 Starboard canard foreplane
8 Refuelling probe forward door
9 Upper IFF antenna
10 Forward-looking infra-red (FLIR)
11 Laser warning receiver
12 Radar equipment bay
13 Air data sensors
14 Port canard foreplane
15 Foreplane diffusion-bonded Titanium structure
16 Hinge mounting trunion
17 Hydraulic actuator
18 Cockpit front pressure bulkhead
19 Control column, full-authority digital active control technology (ACT) fly-by-wire control system
20 Engine throttle levers, HOTAS controls
21 Instrument panel shroud. Smiths Industries full-colour multi-function head-down displays (HDD)
22 GEC Marconi Avionics head-up display (HUD)
23 Frameless windscreen panel
24 Upward hinging cockpit canopy
25 Martin-Baker Mk.16A zero-zero ejection seat
26 Cockpit rear pressure bulkhead
27 Port side console panel
28 Fold-down telescopic boarding ladder
29 Intake boundary-layer diverter
30 Diverter ramp boundary-layer bleed-air spill duct
31 Central intake divider
32 Port engine air intake
33 Intake lip moveable vari-cowl
34 Vari-cowl hydraulic actuators
35 Aft retracting nose undercarriage
36 Hydraulic steering jacks
37 Lower UHF antenna
38 Forward fuselage semi-recessed missile carriage
39 Canopy external release
40 Pressure refuelling connection
41 Intake over-pressure spill duct
42 Cabin air system heat exchanger exhaust
43 Fuselage strake
44 Low-voltage electro-luminescent formation lighting strip
45 Avionics bay access hatch
46 Main avionics equipment bay, port and starboard
47 Avionics/fuel tank bay bulkhead
48 Airbrake hinge mounting
49 Fuselage integral fuel tank, total internal system capacity 1,240 Imp gal (5,640lit)
50 Ventral leading edge slat-drive hydraulic motor
51 Fuel tank dividing bulkhead
52 Gravity fuel fillers
53 Airbrake housing
54 Airbrake hydraulic ram
55 Dorsal airbrake panel, extended
56 Starboard wing missile carriage

57 Leading edge manoeuvring flap, extended
58 Starboard wing tip electronic warfare (EW) equipment pod
59 Starboard navigation light
60 Dual towed radar decoy housing
61 Towed radar decoy
62 Starboard outboard elevon
63 Inboard elevon
64 Starboard wing integral fuel tankage
65 Wing tank fire-suppressant foam filling
66 Strobe light/anti-collision beacon
67 GPS antenna
68 Dorsal spine pipe and cable ducting
69 Intake duct
70 Ventral transverse cannon ammunition magazine
71 Auxiliary power unit (APU)
72 APU exhaust
73 Centre fuselage CFC skin panelling
74 Tank access hatch
75 Main undercarriage wheel bay
76 Hydraulic retraction jack
77 Titanium wing panel root attachment fittings
78 Secondary power system (SPS) equipment bay

79 Accessory equipment gearboxes (2), shaft-driven from engines
80 Engine compressor intake
81 Eurojet EJ200 afterburning low-bypass turbofan
82 Hydraulic reservoirs, dual system
83 Dorsal spine fairing access panels
84 Heat exchanger ram air intake
85 Engine bleed-air primary heat exchanger
86 Main engine mountings
87 Engine bay lining/heat shroud
88 Afterburner ducting
89 Fuel vent valve
90 Fin root attachment fitting
91 Heat exchanger exhaust
92 CFC fin skin panel
93 Leading edge formation lighting strip
94 Fin CFC 'sine-wave' multi-spar structure
95 Fin tip antenna fairing
96 Upper UHF antenna
97 Rear position light
98 Fuel vent
99 Rudder

100 Rudder CFC skin panel with honeycomb substrate
101 Rudder hydraulic actuator
102 Brake parachute housing
103 Hinged parachute door
104 Missile approach warning antenna (MAW)
105 Variable area afterburner nozzle
106 Nozzle hydraulic actuator (4)
107 Nozzle sealing plates
108 Rear fuselage semi-recessed missile carriage
109 Laser warning receiver, above and below
110 Missile carrier/ejector
111 Wing rear spar
112 Emergency arrestor hook
113 Port inboard elevon
114 Inboard elevon CFC structure with honeycomb core

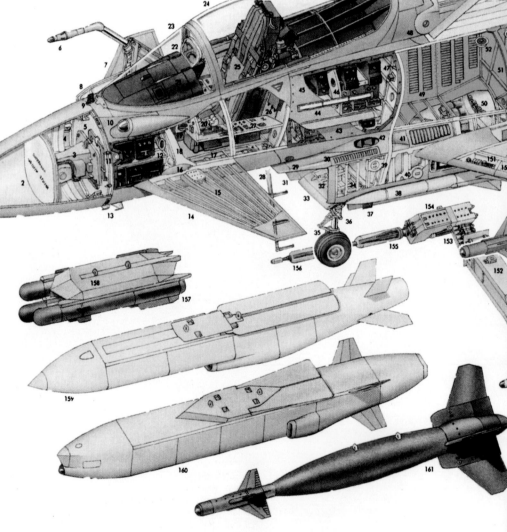

115 Inboard elevon hydraulic actuator
116 Elevon hinge fairing-mounted pyrotechnic launcher and control unit
117 Multi-spar wing panel structure
118 Port wing integral fuel tank
119 Cable conduits
120 CFC skin panelling
121 Outboard elevon hydraulic actuator

126 Wing tip formation lights
127 Port navigation light
128 Equipment cooling ram air intake
129 Forward ECM/ESM antennae
130 AIM-9L Sidewinder, short-range air-to-air missile
131 IRIS-T advanced short-range air-to-air missile
132 Advanced Short-Range Air-to-Air Missile (ASRAAM)
133 Outboard missile pylon
134 Dual missile carrier and launch rails

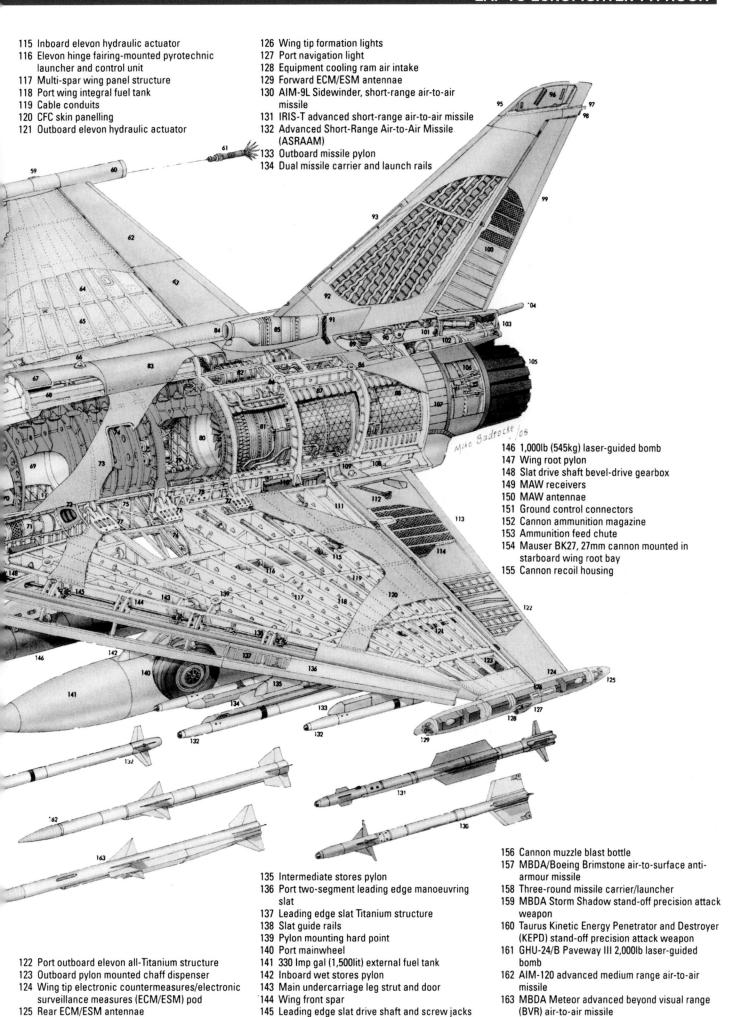

Mike Badrocke/06

146 1,000lb (545kg) laser-guided bomb
147 Wing root pylon
148 Slat drive shaft bevel-drive gearbox
149 MAW receivers
150 MAW antennae
151 Ground control connectors
152 Cannon ammunition magazine
153 Ammunition feed chute
154 Mauser BK27, 27mm cannon mounted in starboard wing root bay
155 Cannon recoil housing

156 Cannon muzzle blast bottle
157 MBDA/Boeing Brimstone air-to-surface anti-armour missile
158 Three-round missile carrier/launcher
159 MBDA Storm Shadow stand-off precision attack weapon
160 Taurus Kinetic Energy Penetrator and Destroyer (KEPD) stand-off precision attack weapon
161 GHU-24/B Paveway III 2,000lb laser-guided bomb
162 AIM-120 advanced medium range air-to-air missile
163 MBDA Meteor advanced beyond visual range (BVR) air-to-air missile

122 Port outboard elevon all-Titanium structure
123 Outboard pylon mounted chaff dispenser
124 Wing tip electronic countermeasures/electronic surveillance measures (ECM/ESM) pod
125 Rear ECM/ESM antennae

135 Intermediate stores pylon
136 Port two-segment leading edge manoeuvring slat
137 Leading edge slat Titanium structure
138 Slat guide rails
139 Pylon mounting hard point
140 Port mainwheel
141 330 Imp gal (1,500lit) external fuel tank
142 Inboard wet stores pylon
143 Main undercarriage leg strut and door
144 Wing front spar
145 Leading edge slat drive shaft and screw jacks

Multi-National F-35

USAF F-35A 5058 at the RIAT Fairford on 10 July 2016. BAE plays a major part in the global F-35 programme producing 13-15% of each aircraft. *(Author)*

The Lockheed Martin F-35 Lightning 2 is stealthy, multi-role strike, reconnaissance and air defence aircraft available in three distinct versions. These are the F-35A Conventional Take Off and Landing (CTOL), the F-35B Short Take Off and Vertical Landing (STOVL) variant and the F-35C Carrier Variant (CV).

The F-35 is a huge international military aircraft programme and it is estimated that over 3,000 will be produced. Lockheed Martin is the main contractor and other major contractors are BAE SYSTEMS, Northrop Grumman and Pratt & Whitney. There is also lesser participation from Italy, Japan, Israel, Korea, Netherlands, Australia, Canada, Denmark, Norway and Turkey. The programme aims to deliver a stealthy, multi-role attack aircraft capable of operating from land and sea.

From its inception, the F-35 or as it was initially known the 'Joint Strike Fighter' was regarded as an international programme to offer a fifth-generation aircraft to nations which could not independently fund such an aircraft. It was primarily designed for air-to-surface but also air-to-air missions. The F-35 incorporates stealth technology and can fly as part of a network for efficient tasking able to deliver weapons effectively and with precision.

BAE's major role in the F-35

BAE has a substantial part to play in the F-35 programme with a 13-15% workshare of each aircraft and when it reaches peak production, it will be worth some £1bn to UK industry alone, with an estimated

RAF F-35B ZM137 hovering in front of the crowds at the RIAT Fairford on 10 July 2016 with the door open behind the pilot for the forward fan. *(Author)*

Rear view of RAF F-35B ZM137 hovering,
showing the exhaust rotated downwards.
(Author)

25,000 UK jobs sustained across more than 500 companies in the supply chain.

BAE Systems has an integral role in the F-35 integrated test force based in Patuxent River, Maryland. More than 30 BAE SYSTEMS' employees are based there, including two test pilots, leading the flight test programme on the F-35B STOVL. The company designs and manufactures the rear aft fuselage and horizontal and vertical tail for all three variants, the wing fold for the F-35C carrier variant (sub-contracted to Canada), and the nozzle bay doors for the F-35B STOVL aircraft. The company provides the Electronic warfare suite, Active interceptor systems, Vehicle management computer and the Electronic components for the communications, navigation and identification system. BAE has design authority on Crew escape, Life support and the Fuel system.

The company is charged with the provision of the facilities for the aircraft at RAF Marham, integration with the Royal Navy's new carrier and UK weapons integration. BAE Systems Australia will provide a heavy airframe maintenance and sustainment capability for the global F-35 fleet in the Southern Pacific region.

When it reaches peak rate production in 2017, the 1,200 workers at BAE Systems' Samlesbury site will be producing one aircraft set each day for shipment to Lockheed Martin's final assembly plant in Fort Worth, Texas. This is a scale of production normally associated with

▼ **F-35A airframe undergoing testing in the BAE Structural and Dynamic Test facility at BAE Brough.**
(BAE Systems)

commercial aircraft manufacture, although the F-35 is a much more complex and advanced product. The UK Government invested £2bn in the F-35 and BAE has invested £150m in its production manufacturing facilities at Samlesbury. At £6.5m for each rear fuselage section it delivers, BAE will earn £20bn on this alone if 3,200 F-35s are built.

F-35 Structural test

An F-35A airframe is undergoing testing in the BAE Structural and Dynamic Test facility at Brough. BAE is responsible for carrying out a large percentage of the structural and fatigue testing required for all three F-35 variants.

The airframe which was delivered in 2009 is connected to a highly complex test

US Marine Corps BF-04's first ski jump on 19 June 2015 flown by BAE's test pilot Peter Wilson. *(BAE Systems)*

rig in which 165 hydraulic actuators replicate the loads the aircraft would experience in flight. The data from the test is captured by 4,000 sensors bonded to the airframe. The test rig has approximately 53 miles of wiring spread around it to connect all the systems and sensors. Each phase of testing, lasting 8,000 hours is equal to the airframe's entire lifetime. Two phases have been completed and the third is in process.

The F-35 in the UK service

The UK had its first view of the F-35 when six arrived at RAF Fairford for the 2016 Royal International Air Tattoo. These were three F-35As, two Marine Corps F-35Bs and a single RAF F-35B serialled ZM137. Though they were based and appeared at Fairford Air Tattoo they were also demonstrated at the Farnborough Air Show.

The UK Government has confirmed orders for 138 F-35Bs, with 23 of them to be available for carrier duties by 2023. Squadron 17(R) which was established on February 2015 is acting as the Operational Evaluation Unit, based Edward Air Force Base in the USA. No 617 Squadron formed of both RAF and RN personnel will be established in January 2018 flying from Marham and the Navy's new aircraft carrier *HMS Queen Elizabeth*. The second squadron will be No. 809 Naval Air Squadron also formed from RAF/RN personnel will be formed in 2023. As the F-35Bs will be able to operate from land bases as well as the Queen Elizabeth Class carriers, it will give UK a truly flexible joint expeditionary Combat Air capability well into the 2030s. The RAF is the lead service for the operation of Lightning 2 but the Joint Lightning 2 Force will be manned by both RAF and RN personnel. In addition to 617 and 809 Naval Air Squadron there will be two more squadrons formed leaving a large number of aircraft for attrition replacements. ∎

On 1 July 2016, a USMC and a RAF F-35B flew over *HMS Queen Elizabeth* being built at Rosyth. *(BAE Systems)*

BAE goes UAV

The Corax URAV (Unmanned Reconnaissance Aerial Vehicle) was fully autonomous from take-off to landing and capable of collecting reconnaissance imagery and transmitting it using very low bandwidth. *(BAE SYSTEMS North West Heritage)*

BAE surprised the media in December 2005, when it exposed its development and trials activities with a UAVs. For some years, BAE had been developing a capability in fully autonomous unmanned airborne systems. These large-scale, fully autonomous UAV platforms enabled it to demonstrate the key technologies for the next generation of airborne systems which include specific programmes in autonomous systems and low observability. Almost amusingly all of BAE's UAVs bar the Taranis have a large notice painted on each side stating, "NO HUMAN OCCUPANT", presumably so that in the event of an accident, rescuers will not hunt for any occupants.

Between 2002 and 2005 the company secretly flew four airframes; the Kestrel, Raven, Corax and Herti. Though the bulk of this work is centred at Warton, the UK company also calls upon UK academia and has expertise in UAVs in two of its other self-styled 'home markets', Australia and the USA.

Kestrel

BAE achieved a UK first when its Kestrel made the maiden flight of a jet-powered unmanned aircraft in UK airspace at remote RAF Machrihanish/Campbeltown Airport on 23 March 2003. Registered G-8-003, Kestrel was a small delta designed to trial a blended body/wing configuration. It had a span of 5.5m and weighed only 140kg. BAE SYSTEMS took the bare airframe, integrated new systems and equally importantly, worked with the Civil Aviation Authority to ensure clearance for the UAV in the UK. Within seven months of the project start, the vehicle was ready to fly. Kestrel also demonstrated the use of advanced low-cost composites and rapid prototyping processes.

Prior to Kestrel BAE had trialled three small radio-controlled machines. Soarer, which came first, was a model glider used to test novel aircraft configurations in 2002. The second, a propeller-driven model called Cap 232, made 30 flights at Samlesbury to test technologies. Then came Hotspot, a jet used for training the Controller and led to CAA permission to flight test Kestrel at Campbeltown.

Raven and Corax

In contrast to Kestrel, the later UAVs designs were taken to Woomera in Australia for their flight testing. Originally conceived as part of the Future Offensive Air System (FOAS) project, the aerodynamically unstable, agile, jet-powered Raven which was built on

Samlesbury. In common with Raven, the Corax is fully autonomous from take-off to landing and capable of collecting reconnaissance imagery and transmitting it using very low bandwidth. Just like Kestrel and Raven the development programme was very short and took only ten months from concept to first flight.

HERTI and Fury

The next UAV development, the HERTI (High Endurance Rapid Technology Insertion) came in three versions all based on Polish motor glider designs. The first, the HERTI 1D was derived from the J5 motor glider but refitted with a jet engine from the Corax. Initial flight trials took place from December 2004 to January 2005 at Woomera. The HERTI 1D was succeeded by the HERTI 1A based on the larger J6 powered glider and powered by a BMW piston engine. On 18 August 2005, the HERTI 1A (registered G-8-008) became the first unmanned aircraft to make a fully autonomous flight, including take-off and landing in the UK. Flying in and out of the remote airfield at Campbeltown, the whole flight was initiated by a click of a mouse!

The more-powerful Rotax-engined HERTI 1B was trialled by the RAF at Camp Bastion in Afghanistan's Helmand province during 2007. It can carry a payload of up to 150kg (330lb), including a full motion video or infrared sensor, plus one fixed narrow field-of-view and two wide field-of-view stills camera. BAE had hoped to receive an urgent operational requirement contract to operate the ➤

◀ **On 18 August 2005, the HERTI 1A (registered G-8-008) became the first unmanned aircraft to make a fully autonomous flight, including take-off and landing in the UK from Campbeltown airport.** *(BAE SYSTEMS North West Heritage)*

▼ **The Fury was an armed version of the HERTI flown at Woomera.** *(BAE Systems)*

Soarer experience first flew at Woomera on 17 December 2003. Incorporating stealth technology, the finless Raven Unmanned Combat Aerial Vehicle (UCAV) tested vehicle control concepts. Raven carried out several highly successful flights and was fully autonomous from take-off to landing. It was followed by a second prototype in November 2004. (The Future Offensive Air System programme was tasked with developing a replacement for the Royal Air Force's Tornado GR4 strike aircraft. It was cancelled in 2005.)

Demonstrating rapid engineering process, the Raven was followed little over a year later by Corax URAV (Unmanned Reconnaissance Aerial Vehicle) which drew on much of the technology developed for the Raven. It re-used much of the Raven; the fuselage, engine and undercarriage, married to a new composite wing built BAE Systems' advanced manufacturing facility at

HERTI over Afghanistan, but this failed to materialise. An armed version of the HERTI was developed and flown at Woomera called the Fury which could carry a lightweight missile. One of the HERTIs was registered as G-HERT by BAE in November 2007 but was deregistered at the end of 2014 as withdrawn from use.

Mantis

Under a contract awarded by the UK MOD in July 2008, BAE Systems was appointed as the industry lead and prime contractor of a jointly funded project to develop a world-class Advanced Concept Technology Demonstrator (ACTD) UAV called Mantis. Whereas BAE's earlier UAVs had all been small, the Mantis is of larger proportions and is 65ft long, fitted with two Rolls-Royce RB250B-17 engines. First flight was on 21st October 2009 at Woomera, again demonstrating BAE's rapid engineering processes. The twin turboprop-powered aircraft made a number of flights from Woomera, demonstrating its ISTAR (information, surveillance, target acquisition, and reconnaissance) potential. It is a concept demonstrator with a viable mission system and is intended to be fully autonomous. A model of the Mantis was exhibited with a representative combat load of four Paveway precision-guided bombs and two Brimstone-like air-to-surface missiles. Mantis returned to BAE Warton in June 2010 but has not flown again.

BAE Jetstream G-BWWW which is a surrogate UAV testbed, together with the BAE Mantis, ZK210, a twin turboprop UAV seen at Warton. G-BWWW now has an all black livery. *(BAE SYSTEMS)*

⌃ BAE Mantis, ZK210 first flew at Woomera in Australia on 21st October 2009. It made a number of flights from there demonstrating its ISTAR (information, surveillance, target acquisition, and reconnaissance) potential. It returned to Warton in 2010 and has not flown since then. *(BAE Systems)*

The BAE SYSTEMS/Cranfield University Demon made the first flight of an aircraft without moving flying controls allowed by the UK Civil Aviation Authority on 17 September 2010. It is a very small jet-powered demonstrator weighing 90kgs with wingspan of 2.5m. *(BAE Systems)*

Demon

Demon, a combined development of BAE and Cranfield University, is a UAV designed to fly without using conventional elevators or ailerons, using jet blasts of air blown over the trailing edges of its wings to manoeuvre. The small jet-powered demonstrator which weighs approximately 90kgs has a wingspan of just 2.5m made from carbon-fibre. It made the first flight of an aircraft without moving flying controls allowed by the UK Civil Aviation Authority on 17 September 2010 from Walney Island. Because it is designed to fly with no conventional elevators or ailerons, getting its pitch and roll control from blown air, it requires fewer moving parts, making it easier to maintain and repair. Demon can fly parts of its mission by itself but, as it is currently an experimental vehicle and is not fully autonomous unlike the MANTIS.

The challenge for BAE would be to

BAE Jetstream ASTRAEA trials

Many of these autonomous systems are being developed using the company's Jetstream 31 G-BWWW which functions as a surrogate UAV testbed, where the on-board pilots can take their hands off the controls and hand over control to the on-board system developed by the ASTRAEA team. The ASTRAEA (Autonomous Systems Technology Related Airborne Evaluation and Assessment) programme is designed to allow UAVs to fly safely through classes of airspace safely without special restrictions of operation. BAE is one of seven aerospace companies involved in UK industry-led ASTRAEA. BAE's test programme is critical to helping the UK reach its target. Admittedly it has a vested interest, as currently it can only test Taranis in Australia. Proving it could be flown safely in the UK would speed up development and lower costs.

During 2012 the Jetstream began a series of more than 20 flights demonstrating its capabilities while operating in shared airspace. Onboard control systems mean it can fly as if it were a UAV without any input from the pilots. The ASTRAEA system is designed to prevent mid-air collisions with other aircraft using a 'sense and avoid' system, detecting and avoiding bad weather conditions and relaying air traffic control instructions to the remote pilot via satellite to the ground control station.

In April 2013, G-BWWW flew on a circuitous route from BAE Warton to Inverness. It was the first flight in UK airspace by a full-sized UAV controlled by a remote pilot at Warton with the aircraft making its own routine decisions. (There was a human pilot on board in the event of emergency). There were no passengers, but the 16-seater aircraft flew in airspace shared with passenger airliners during the 500-mile journey.

BAE made the maiden flight of its low-observable UCAV technology demonstrator, Taranis ZZ250 at Woomera 13 August 2013. Taranis is approximately the same size as the Hawk trainer and is also powered by an Adour 951 engine. *(BAE Systems)*

produce a full-scale aircraft with this technology and incorporating it into an aircraft with a stealthy design.

BAE Kingfisher

In Australia, BAE engineers have been trialling an Intelligent Landing System for UAVs to land themselves. Kingfisher is a small UAV constructed for the specific purpose of autonomously locating suitable landing strips in an emergency and landing without relying on GPS, remote piloting, special ground equipment, earlier survey of the site or other external systems. With such systems, UAVs can quickly incorporate other landing sites. The system brings the UAV in on a normal approach so it can share the airstrip with other, normal traffic.

BAE Taranis

In July 2010 BAE unveiled its low-observable UCAV technology demonstrator, Taranis to the aviation media at Warton. Taranis is a UK-only technology demonstrator, with BAE Systems heading a joint MoD/industry team. It is jointly funded by BAE and the MoD. Taranis is approximately the same size as the Hawk trainer and is also powered by an Adour 951 engine, but there the similarity ends. Most of the systems and structure were designed by BAE but some parts, for example the undercarriage, from the Saab Gripen are off-the-shelf items.

Taranis underwent a long period of ground testing before transport to Woomera. Painted grey with low-visibility RAF roundels and serialled ZZ250, its 15-minute maiden flight took

▲ Another photo of Taranis ZZ250 with its under-carriage retracted showing its low-observable profile. *(BAE Systems)*

▼ A great lineage - the shape of a Spitfire Mk IX, with Typhoon FGR4 ZK358 and Taranis ZZ250 at Warton. *(BAE Systems)*

place on 13 August 2013. Three successful flight test phases have taken place so far with the third of these ending in autumn 2015. BAE hopes a fourth set of flight trials may take place and Taranis is being maintained in flight-ready condition at Warton.

BAE states that Taranis "incorporates world-leading stealth technologies, propulsion systems, all of which have direct relevance to the next-generation of military aerospace capabilities. Taranis was designed to demonstrate our ability to create a system capable of undertaking sustained surveillance, marking targets, gathering intel, deterring adversaries and carrying out strikes in hostile territory". BAE indicated that more than 1.5m man-hours had been invested in the Taranis programme. It is a highly sensitive

programme and little has been revealed about it, for example, no information has been given about the UAV's performance and some aspects of the design remain classified. Other firms contributing to Taranis include Rolls-Royce, Claverham, Cobham and QintetiQ.

While Taranis is a UK-only programme, the development of a UCAV by a joint BAE/Dassault programme for a FCAS (Future Combat Air System) is covered by the 2014 Anglo-French strategic defence agreement. This is intended to lead in 2025 to operationally representative demonstrators and an operational vehicle after 2030 with a 50ft wingspan and two internal weapons bays. This is the most advanced programme of its kind in Europe and has a joint investment budget of €2bn. ■